First published in 1989 by
DIYMAN, I.o.M.

ISBN 0 9514751 0 X

Printed by
Print Centres Limited,
Isle of Man

By the same author:

EVADER. **Wartime escape.**
FOLK DOCTOR'S ISLAND. **Witchcraft & unorthodox healing.**

CONTENTS

Chapter		Page
1	First Sight	7
2	A Mayflower Sailing	11
3	Restoration	14
4	Getting On With It	20
5	Moving In	24
6	The First Born	28
7	Gaining Ground	32
8	The Food Factory	35
9	Solid Sally	39
10	Fuel	45
11	More Fuel	49
12	Self-Sufficiency	53
13	Fresh and Free	58
14	Larry The Lamb	63
15	On The Quayside	67
16	Into Business	71
17	Les Lapins	75
18	A New Marshall	80
19	Mad Sunday	85
20	Race Week	89
21	Piglets	94
22	The Market	98
23	End of Season	101
24	Charlie Drake	105
25	La Cuisine	109
26	Noel	113
27	Fruit and Vegetables	117
28	Reclamation	121
29	Family Affairs	125
30	Food For Thought	129
31	Funny Bunny	133
32	In The Smoke	137
33	Traders' Tales	141
34	At Work And Play	145

35	Breakaway	150
36	Never Again	154
37	Home Again	158
38	Love On The Farm	161
39	A Bad Year	166
40	The Only Solution	171
41	The Count-Down	175
42	Pee-Co	179
43	Breaking Point	185
44	A Decade Is Over	190

ISLAND

OF

DREAMS

Denys Teare

CHAPTER 1

FIRST SIGHT

WE stopped the car on the country roadside to forcibly drag open a heavy, dilapidated old gate, that had once swung freely between two large, impressive, whitewashed pillars, built long ago of local stone.

The periodic renewals of whitewash had been sadly absent for many years and, through the gateway, the lane was so thickly lined with trees and neglected holly bushes that a network of leaves and branches intermingled overhead. Then, within this natural rustic framework we had our first glimpse of "Ballaneddin".

The estate agent had spoken of, "A farmhouse needing renovation, several outbuildings and thirty acres of hillside, overgrown with gorse and bracken".

First impressions can be so misleading, but I only needed one sideways glance at Fay to realise that she was already thinking, "This is it, this can become our ideal home". By the time I'd parked the hired car she was already visualising attractive curtains at those Georgian windows, roses growing around a gaily painted front door and was eagerly waiting to see the layout of the interior.

My own initial observations however had immediately taken in the very dubious condition of the sagging roof, complete absence of guttering, the many broken windows within the rotting frames and coupled these visual defects with the advance knowledge that there was no electricity, no gas, no mains water supply and only a primitive "bucket and chuck it" form of sanitation.

The turning of the rusted lock caused slight delay, or so it seemed in our eagerness to go inside, it would have been quicker to try the rear entrance, for the back door was hanging dejectedly off its hinges anyhow.

Once inside, we found that apart from normal deterioration, aided enthusiastically by a legion of woodworms and various forms of fungi, very little change had taken place for at least half a century.

The cooking range stood cold and rusty in the kitchen, the dampened wallpaper in the parlour bore patterns of a bygone fashion and the surviving window panes showed bubbles and blemishes totally unacceptable by today's manufacturing standards.

The walls were two feet thick and would retain the cosy warmth from peat and timber glowing in the open firegrates but would maintain a necessary coolness for the dairy, with its stone flagged floor and tiny window openings.

The bedrooms were bare; rain had penetrated through walls and ceilings. A further stairway led to dark windowless attics, but this was so very worm eaten that I had to tightly grip the banister rail and gingerly place my feet at the extreme sides of each tread, for the centres would not have taken my weight.

The attic floor was partly boarded but I did not venture right across lest I should drop through and abruptly stop astride a joist. *[That certainly would have spoilt my day.]*

Outside in the farmyard I wandered round various outbuildings, all with the same thick stone walls and slate roofs. There were stables with cobblestoned floors, and harness still hung amongst the cobwebs on the walls. Standing room for at least half a dozen milkers that was very far removed from present day hygienic milking parlour requirements. Plus store houses, lofts and a pair of pig styes, each with its opening through the wall to pour the swill straight into the stone-lined troughs.

At the rear of the house was a row of beehives and goose boxes also built in stone. Close to the back door was a building which ran partly into the hillside, its slate roof lined below with timber. There were shelves all round and it bore signs of having been whitewashed very many times. This I suppose would have been the cold storage area for cream, cheeses and salted meats.

For any couple who wanted to enjoy a country life away from the pressures of modern living, getting that bit nearer to nature, then surely here must be an absolutely ideal setting. Fay had been born on a small farm in Scotland and with one of those womanly intuitions, for which there is no explanation, she announced that this was a friendly house, had a healthy atmosphere of much happiness and laughter that could very easily ring out again.

Ballaneddin is situated on that enchanting little island in the Irish sea loved by so many holidaymakers and people in retirement, the Isle of Man, and this was of very special significance to myself, for, although we had flown across from England earlier that morning I was actually back in the land of my forefathers.

With its Puff-Puff railway and horse-drawn trams the island has wonderful charm and tranquility and is splendid for the upbringing of children but, for the ambitious school leaver the opportunities have been very limited, unless he left the island. Consequently, many of this tiny nation have become seafarers, several with great distinction, others have settled in various parts of the globe where their families are still proud of the Manx three-legged emblem and their membership of the World Manx Association.

My own family's quest for employment had initially extended only to England but, my surname is so basically Manx, that even in North America several years ago, on giving my name I was surprisingly confronted with the question "*Kanys ta shiu?*" to which I was pleased to quickly reply "*Braew, braew, kanys ta shiu hene?*" but at this point the conversation seemed to reach a standstill for with this *how-do-you-do* salutation the Canadian and I had just about reached our limit in the Manx native Gaelic. Most Manx folk can manage to use a few phrases and each year all new laws are proclaimed to the public in both Manx and English in an open-air ceremony that has been taking place for about a thousand years.

Ballaneddin is mentioned as far back as 1515 in the Manorial Roll, a sort of Manx Doomsday Book, written at that time as "*Balley yn eddan*" meaning, in it's simplest form "farm of the stream", but I have read that the "*neddan, feddan*" incorporated with a place name indicates a narrow stream running down a deep channel like a pipe. This is interesting, for, at the rear of the house the land rises steeply and at five hundred feet above sea level one can still see the remains of a fortification from pre-Christian times and just nearby, on Ballaneddin land, there is a fresh-water spring amongst the heather, with a stone surround forming a small cistern, from which water is actually piped underground all the way down the hillside to the cattle trough in the farmyard. Later I was to learn that the lead pipe of today had been laid eighty years previously to replace very old wooden channels.

Near to the back-door of the farmhouse, across the stone-flagged yard was a low roofed building with a chimney and an old washing boiler still bricked in position. The washing day procedure would have involved not only securing an ample supply of dry timber for burning, but also the carrying of many bucketfuls of water from the cattle trough, past the stables, past the shippen, and all round the back of the house. The mountain water was still running into the trough with just a partition and a covering slate to differentiate between livestock and domestic usage.

The estate agent began to apologise, "I've a feeling that I might have brought you over on a wasted journey" he said, when he realised the dilapidated state of the property he was offering but before that day was over he had been handed a deposit.

WE WERE GOING TO LIVE AT BALLANEDDIN!

CHAPTER 2

A *MAYFLOWER* SAILING

IT is unfortunate that for so many people the mere thought of the Isle of Man and up pops in their mind a little ticket saying "Tax haven". This is certainly of considerable importance if you happen to be in a particularly high income bracket and have become so sickened by the rate of taxation claimed against you that you are prepared to forsake your homeland and to take up residence off-shore, for, although the Island is actually regarded as one of the British Isles, it is not specifically a member of the United Kingdom . . . *vive-la-différence.*

The Island's low taxation system is indeed enjoyed by the several millionaires who take advantage by being in residence, and the Manx Government in turn must be happy to receive more revenue from such individuals than from large numbers of average Manx breadwinners put together.

The benefits of the complete absence of death duties are frequently quoted; but it does not necessarily mean that everyone dies in the Isle of Man with a smile on their face, for you still "can't take it with you".

The vast majority of the people living upon the Island are there very simply because they just don't know anywhere else that can offer the welfare security of medical, educational and police services that are not understaffed but operate with courtesy and efficiency amid such scenic beauty and in a general atmosphere of well-being amongst friendly, homely, law-abiding citizens.

I considered myself very fortunate indeed to be taking Ballaneddin and was grateful for the 'phone call of the previous day telling me that a neglected farm had just become available on the market. Particularly as we had established that the vendor was willing to allow the balance to remain outstanding for an indefinite period on payment of interest only. Building Societies did not operate in the Isle of Man at that time but this private arrangement would enable us to carry out a complete farm house renovation with what cash we had available and at the same time allow the opportunity to look round carefully for some appropriate means of earning a living. The prospect of an agricultural livelihood solely from the overgrown hillside was certainly not a viable proposition but we would put the outbuildings to their best advantage and certainly a supply of fresh eggs and goatsmilk would form a valuable contribution to the family economy.

Only twenty-two days later all the farewells and goodbyes had been spoken, hands had been shaken and the many faces and voices that had once formed part of our daily routine of life were to become features of annual visits only, for, we had now stepped aboard the boat that was to take us to our chosen island. The mooring ropes had been released and we were already easing away from the Liverpool dockside.

A small group of relatives had come along to wave their final gestures of bon-voyage, though not quite with the solemnity of a *Mayflower* send off. This was a sort of "*go west young man*" though not very far west, nor really all that young.

There was however, one young man on board who would not remember this day's sailing, regardless of its significance. He was our Tony, just a little bundle in Fay's arms, on his way to a beautiful little island which would become the only home he would remember.

The propellers churned up the inky Mersey water and the seventy-five mile voyage was under way, that was to take us right down the river estuary, passing all the clanging marker buoys and out into the open sea.

For Fay and I, life had not been exactly trouble-free these recent years, we'd each been shattered by the failure of previous teenage sweetheart marriages. But now, we had embarked upon an entirely new phase in our lives. We were both just so happy that we kept exchanging glances and grinning like a couple of youngsters as all the tension and anxieties we'd known in the past drained right away.

By mid-day we were out of sight of land and made our way along the deck to the dining room, where we wined and dined in celebration.

The more usual and indeed more economic procedure would have been the consumption of home-made sandwiches and we laughed together as I recalled that there had once been an occasion when I had happened to make a visit to the Island alone.

After a couple of hours at sea, the gentleman seated directly opposite me had put down his newspaper and poured himself hot coffee from a thermos flask. I decided the time had come for me too to take refreshment and produced a very similar flask, knowing it contained a good homemade vegetable soup. Screwing off the cap I filled it with the first delicious portion, very acceptable indeed, but when I tried to pour a refill there was no more liquid, the wholesome body of the soup was now all semi-solid.

Have you ever tried to eat a hot, thick vegetable purée out of a thermos flask, on board a rolling ship, USING A PENKNIFE?

CHAPTER 3

RESTORATION

WE'D made a big decision by taking on the challenge of a semi-derelict farm house, especially as our sum of available capital was rather modest in comparison with the assets of those incoming tax-exiles settling upon the Isle of Man.

We were entering upon an entirely new phase of our existence, the prime concern being basic simplicity, having already learnt that the sophisticated manner of business success and financial gain does not necessarily bear an advantageous relationship with either health or domestic happiness.

Now, it was to be a re-start, almost from scratch with all bitter resentment of past injustice to be overcome. I'd no occupation to go to, no pension and no immediate idea whatsoever of how to produce an income but all this was to be outweighed purely by enthusiasm and willingness to enjoy and enter into the style of life on the enchanting Island.

Drawing upon our joint resources of experience and common sense, well, surely some idea was bound to turn up. To quote Fay's words . . . "Denys has done many things, but he's got lots of brains that he hasn't even used yet". How complimentary can a woman be?

Until Ballaneddin had been made reasonably fit for occupation we were to live seven miles away, in a tiny fisherman cottage, behind the Lifeboat House and said to be the oldest property in the port of Ramsey. Much smaller than the farmhouse but with the same traditional thick stone walls, low ceilings and small windows, but ever so snug and homely.

Our next journey into the country was to take a more detailed look around our proposed dream home, and see just what sort of worm eaten shambles we'd voluntarily hung about our necks.

Had we allowed ourselves to be carried away with a romantic ideal that had been viewed through rose coloured specs.?

If it really had such great potential, why hadn't some other couple snatched it off the market.

Just as soon as we turned off the roadway and into the tree lined drive again all our doubts were dismissed completely, this was to be our new home and we were to take up the way of life of our choice.

Along the highway ran supplies of electricity, mains water and the telephone cable, which could all be laid underground for the one hundred yards or so as far as the house. Our driveway was good and firm with a stone surface that had been consolidated by the hoofs of horses and wheels of carts led along by many generations of earlier residents. Fortunately the owner of the adjoining field was willing to allow a trench to be taken out in a parallel line leaving our attractive approach road undisturbed.

Now it was a matter of co-ordinating the hire of an excavator with the availability of the Electricity Board, the Water Authority and the Telephone Engineers. The timing was perfect, the trench was opened up one day then filled in and levelled off the next, a forty-eight hour operation that had brought the old world farmstead right into the twentieth century.

While the excavator was on the premises there was the septic tank area to be dug out and trenches for the soak-aways to be cut.

In front of the house stood a large yew tree, so picturesque, but so deadly, for all the varieties of British yew tree are extremely poisonous. Some livestock can die within minutes of eating the toxic foliage so we certainly did not wish to take any risk with our baby boy crawling round beneath its branches. I contacted the Forestry Board, for their permission is required for the removal of any tree over a certain circumference; permission was duly granted so, with the other jobs completed, the excavator was now directed towards the yew tree. The metal claw groped into the ground around the base, removing great scoopfuls of earth and snapping through the roots then, with a hydraulic push it was toppled over. Just a few minutes action by machine that could have taken me many hours by hand. I had chatted with the young plant hire operator while he had a lunch break and was quite intrigued to watch him peel a large onion, cut it in slices, lay it on bread, and then smear it all over with black treacle; when I mentioned this unusual combination to Fay that evening she immediately recalled it as her mother's remedy for colds.

During that afternoon an elderly gentleman arrived by bicycle.

"Pleased to meet you", he said "I'm Jackie Teare, Ballaneddin".

This was puzzling, but then I remembered that in times gone by it was not unusual for a farmer's eldest son to marry and set up his home nearby but still be recognised under the farming name, in this particular case there was a further Ballaneddin just the width of one field away. The fact that it was occupied by a household with the same Manx family name as myself was pure coincidence.

The duplication of farm names had taken place long before the introduction of a postal service so I offered to quote my address as Ballaneddin (West) and avoid confusion. Jackie peddled away but returned in a little while to introduce his son, who carried with him a petrol driven chain saw and in a short space of time the old yew tree was reduced into log sizes that just needed splitting with a heavy axe for use inside the open firegrate. This was a kind neighbourly act which I certainly appreciated and although in the years to come we would sometimes go for weeks without making contact, it was always comforting to know that just across the field good neighbours were on hand.

A close examination inside the attic area, using a flash-light and sticking a penknife blade into the timbers revealed that any attempted repair-and-make-do approach would be far too short sighted, what I needed was some contractor to quote a price for the complete stripping off and renewal of the entire roof, before any work whatsoever be undertaken lower down.

Soon I was to learn that most of the smaller building firms already had sufficient work in hand at that time of the year and could not offer a starting date for at least a couple of months. Whereas the larger concerns were quite content to erect their rows of retirement bungalows and showed little interest in taking a "one-off" roofing job way out in the country.

Had there been more capital available of course, the entire restoration could have been placed in the hands of an architect who, for his professional fee, would have negotiated contracts with concerns who specialised in such projects, would have carried out supervision and inspection, and would have issued certificates for payment stage by stage.

I had applied to the Local Government Board for permission to install a septic tank system which would, in due course, be subjected to their official inspection but, beyond that, I myself was to be the architect, surveyor, building inspector, site manager, clerk of works, general labourer and, unfortunately, paymaster general.

Luckily, some young fellows had recently formed a company

and their roof quotation was, not only quite acceptable, but they undertook to start work within the week.

One of the earliest pitfalls that awaits a householder negotiating with members of the building trade is their absolute unwillingness to offer any precise date for completion. With possible shortage of materials and labour complications the builder's outlook is quite understandable, but it is wretchedly frustrating if, after a few days of demolition work have ensured that you are now at their mercy, the work force just doesn't turn up one morning and you then learn that they are busily engaged on the other side of the village, pulling someone else's house to pieces.

Anyhow, there must be mutual respect and confidence shown, for so many people expect tradesmen to perform miracles, which are a bit difficult under any circumstances, but even more so on a building site, when the chaps are wondering whether the customer will display the same amount of speed and enthusiasm he requires when his own turn comes, at the time to write out a cheque in settlement of the account.

I offered weekly payments based on the actual work carried out, an arrangement that was very willingly accepted, so quite soon scaffolding was erected and the old damaged slates began to be stripped off, allowing daylight to stream into the attic for the first time since those many years ago when the house had been constructed.

Huge baulks of timber formed the roof trusses, with interesting joint formations that are no longer in general use. Each piece still bore a number, chiselled on the side, for every truss would first of all have been manufactured and assembled in some joiner's workshop, numbered, taken apart, then brought out into the country by horse and cart to be reassembled in its present position, where hardwood pegs had been driven through, keying each joint tightly together.

Some trusses had remained strong and sound to the present day and were to be retained but, still more interesting, was the realisation that some of those old timbers had known an even previous usage as masts of sailing ships. One could very easily conjure up all sorts of possible background stories. Had they been salvaged from wreckage washed up on the nearby beach, or further round the rocky coastline, after a night of storm? Had they once vibrated to the roar of cannon fire, known piracy, or, much more probable, helped in the smuggling activities for which the Island was once so renowned?

It was no use standing amongst the rafters, looking out to sea and daydreaming for, with our proposed dream home now standing like a ruin, exposed to the open sky, there was a certain amount of urgency about the situation. Although the old stone walls were so thick, a heavy downpour of rain onto the recently revealed top surfaces would wash away the crumbling clay and lime that was holding them together. Some such buildings in the neighbourhood had been left unprotected over a series of winters and were now reduced to a mere pile of stones.

The work was carried out in good time and in a very satisfactory manner, though it was only after the job had started did I learn that the particular joiner in charge had a very good reputation throughout the trade for his accuracy and conscientious ability, so, now that the building was more or less weatherproof, a price was agreed for the attic floor to be stripped out and replaced, using new joists that would be left exposed below to form an attractive feature of the bedroom ceilings.

The tiny glass panes of the Georgian style windows contributed much towards the attractive exterior character of the building and needed to be retained, some of which were original bottle-bottom pieces utilised for economy at the time but now in demand to introduce olde-worlde-charm into brand new structures. Most of the window frames were found to be completely beyond repair and had to be reproduced in a Ramsey workshop. Within the hollow boxwork which surrounds that type of fixture, the pulley-wheels and sash weights had long since ceased to perform their function. So the rotting, worm eaten sections were all stripped out and replaced by solid timber, onto which I would fit, at a later date, the modern but inconspicuous coil springing to give the windows their traditional up and down sashway movements.

Every day, as work progressed, great bonfires were lit to dispose of all the diseased and potentially contagious woodwork and

there was the liberal application of a liquid from a large container clearly labled "Extra Strong Woodworm Killer" which I hoped would deal with every Pocket Hercules of the insect world.

The services of an electrician were incorporated into the operation and work proceeded with the temporary refinement of one bare electric light bulb that could be dangled on a wire from various nails strategically hammered into the wooden beams throughout the building. Then, having been given a recommendation, I endeavoured to trace the whereabouts of the "midnight plumber". There are many humorous nick-names in daily use upon the Island but this one was quite intriguing, for his workmanship was said to be very good but he invariably made arrangements to have access to a property after all other tradesmen had finished for the day, when he would work alone and partway through the night, a sort of Lone (kitchen) Ranger.

Eventually I made contact, a price was agreed, a bathroom suite and kitchen units chosen, together with a system of central heating whereby hot water would be pumped to radiators in different rooms via tiny micro-bore piping, said to be very successful in the Scandinavian countries.

He seemed to be a pleasant young fellow and I wondered why he appeared to scorn the company of his countrymen, but later on, I was to meet his attractive wife who was a cabaret singer, he would work while she sang until the early hours of the morning when, he would put away his tools and drive to pick her up and take her home.

With usual building site humour and legpulling we all worked happily together, getting on well with the job and generally sharing a few well-earned pints together at the end of each week. The geographical position brought about the inevitable, time-worn Irish stories. Did you know that Paddy invented the lavatory seat? But a Manxman thought of putting a hole in it!

CHAPTER 4

GETTING ON WITH IT

THE dilapidated old farm house had begun to look worse and worse, as we reduced it to the appearance of an absolute ruin. Then, gradually, as the roof was completed, the window frames refitted, floors boarded and a new staircase placed into position, what had been an empty shell, full of broken slates, dust, and grit from perished plaster and flaked whitewash from the walls, now began to reveal its true potential.

Fay concerned herself very much with the layout for her kitchen — which had previously been the stone flagged dairy — and with the positioning of lights, switches and power points throughout a building that had never known electricity.

All the crumbling plaster had been hacked away from the walls, so now I needed a tradesman's skill to replace it. Plasterers around the north of the Island all seemed to be fully employed at that time of the year. In any case it is far easier for a man to skim over plasterboard and brand new brickwork in a modern building than to tackle the old uneven stone walls of Ballaneddin, where sometimes two or even three layers of sand and cement mixture would be needed to bring out a reasonably level surface before any plaster could be used at all.

Our electrician spoke of a couple of plasterers being available in Laxey, on the other side of the Island, and he quoted the public house they used. This was important for, to negotiate the services of casual workers in the building trade, the names of pubs sometimes proved more productive than residential addresses. On the Island all tradesmen are required to register themselves with the government, and such registration is only accepted on production of qualifications, consequently, when hiring labour, one should be less likely to start a fellow on the job and then find that he does not know what he's doing.

We agreed a payment on an hourly basis, materials were delivered to the site and soon the rough, uneven stones, the wiring and the pipework were being smoothed out of sight and the squareness of the rooms took shape.

Only in one of the ground floor rooms had anyone ever trodden upon the luxury of wooden boarding, this was now rotten and below it I found lots of walnut shells, from the tree that grew alongside the house. The three letter name of the rodents who had put them there is never spoken by the more superstitious families of the Island for fear of misfortune. You speak of "long tails" or "queer fellows" and everyone knows exactly what you mean and I think its better to bear respect for the beliefs and feelings of one's fellow men, rather than court disaster.

A more widely known procedure in the Isle of Man is the bidding of a courteous "Good-day fairies" to ensure well-being when driving over a certain bridge not far from the airport. Even if you don't believe in fairies, the courtesy costs you nothing, so why take any chances?

Several tons of wet, freshly mixed concrete were delivered to the front of the house and piped through the doorway, straight into the hall, where it was hastily spread and levelled throughout all the rooms of the ground floor area.

When this was completely hard and dry an arrangement was made whereby a large mobile tar boiler was towed along to the house. A fire was lit inside the machine at four in the morning to get the huge vat of moulten pitch ready for spreading and by the end of the day the floor in each room was covered from wall to wall with a hard, damp-proof, antiseptic smelling carpet of black asphalt.

Now that the shovelling of rubble, carrying of planks and ladders had been mostly concluded it was safe to start puttying the one hundred or so squares of glass into the Georgian windows, plus a rather fine looking coloured and leaded piece that I had managed to bring home from an auction which, with a little gentle persuasion, made an attractive feature in a window frame halfway up the stairs.

Outside each window I used slates to form the traditional style of window sill that would deflect the rain away from the walls and, now that the building was weatherproof, the time had come for the adding of such refinements as doors, skirting boards and banister rails. Eventually there came the moment when, at the turn of a tap, water flowed and we felt that we had at last created a brand new house within the old shell and yet managed to retain the charm and character of a bygone era.

The Island takes great care to guard its reputation for complete absence of certain animal diseases and, at the time of our departure from Liverpool there had been an outbreak of the dreaded foot and mouth disease in England. Consequently, our two family pets, Twiggy, the faithful bulldog bitch, and our tortoise-shell tailless cat were compelled to stay behind in Cheshire until it would be declared safe for the transport of livestock to the Island again.

Various forms of wildlife that had ventured into the deserted farm had moved away as the reconstruction progressed, the hedgehog with her nest of babies that we used to peep at was no longer there, one sleepy little bat that I found in the barn, looking like some tiny mouse wearing folded wings was no longer there, and I've seen none since. There is an abundance of birdlife, the wood pigeons and magpies are in such great numbers that there is a Government bounty on their heads. The more that one shoots, the more heads can be taken along to Ramsey in gruesome little packages where twelve bore cartridges are freely exchanged pro-rata.

There are no foxes whatsoever on the Island but there must be quite a large number of the Manx polecats, judging by the many times I've seen their corpses on the roadside. They don't look anything like a pussy cat, more like a stoat, or large ferret, with sandy coloured fur and a length from tip to tail of up to a yard.

The workmen had now all been paid off but there was still a lot that we would do ourselves. There was rain water guttering and down-spouts to be fitted all round, there was shelving to be built, plastering to be finished off, archways and alcoves to be completed and the tiling of the kitchen and the bathroom.

The winter set in while we were drying out the building (if you do this too quickly the plaster all cracks) and on New Year's Day we built our sitting room fireplace. Near the front of the house had been a small stone structure that seemed to have housed geese or ducks at one time but was no longer worthy of repair. Fay dislodged the stonework piece by piece and steered them through the front door on a wheel barrow, where they were repositioned to form a quite artistic feature, in spire of the handicap that although our baby Tony had by now achieved his first few faltering steps unassisted, he preferred to spend time crawling through my mixed cement, or actually sitting in it.

Our next joint operation was the thorough cleaning out of the building, from top to botton, all the sand, grit, plaster and wood shavings had to be got rid of, prior to painting.

There were the doorframes, the architraves, the skirtings and the window frames, all to be primed, knotted, undercoated and gloss painted. Every wall of every room in the house had its newly plastered surface covered twice with emulsion paint, gallons and gallons of it, but the most time consuming areas had surely been the ceilings. Exposed wooden beams look so picturesque and homely within the right dwelling, but bare timber joists need many hours of tedious sanding, staining and varnishing to reach the desired effect.

The restoration of our farm house became at last completed, the operation had at times been quite physically exhausting, but always so mentally exhilarating.

Our dream home was now ready for occupation, just ten busy months since we had first sighted that rather dismal, dilapidated 'Ballaneddin'.

CHAPTER 5

MOVING IN

WE had been very happy to live in the fisherman's cottage and been so pleased to get to know the interesting personalities who gain a livelihood around the quayside.

Never had we enjoyed such an abundance of fresh fish, sometimes the plaice we ate had been actually alive and flapping when brought into our tiny kitchen, maybe half an hour earlier.

Other days there might be shellfish available such as fresh crabs, or "queenie" scollops but the simplest and to me one of the most acceptable shellfood dishes was *moules mariniere.*

I simply had to check the tide table for the precise time and day of the next spring tide, when the water would be at its lowest level, and take a bucket beneath the old Victorian pier that carried a single track railway line almost half a mile away from the shore. Within easy reach I could then take my requirements from the thousands upon thousands of living mussels, attached to the iron pillars, which would be taken home and left to stand in water outside the back door overnight while they emptied themselves.

A sharp little knife removed all barnacles and beards before the shells were taken into the kitchen where, some chopped onion, a splash of wine, a little expertise and a few minutes in the pan produced a delicacy we could enjoy quite often. The name is misleading: those spring tides take place every month of the year, just when the terrestial attaction of both moon and sun coincide.

We both had very healthy appetites and thoroughly enjoyed good quality food, Fay's greatest satisfaction was in the preparation and presentation of superb home cooked creations and this was to play an important part in our future almost self-sufficient lifestyle.

Many a time, after working all day in the wind and the rain on the building site, I had made my way along the side of the harbour, round to the back of the lifeboat station, then, closing the cottage door to keep the howling wind behind me, I would settle down in candlelight to a glass of wine and some exquisite dish which, though knowing I'm so obviously biased, I believe could not have been bettered in the most exclusive hotels of Europe.

The serenity of the evening could however, be shattered by an unexpected "BOOM!" Followed a few seconds later by yet another as emergency rockets exploded high above the rooftops. Then we knew that some of the fellows with whom we had often drunk so heartily and sang so lustily would each be driving, peddling or running to risk their own lives onboard the lifeboat and the words *for those in peril on the sea* took a very realistic and rather chilling significance.

Each Monday morning a livestock auction takes place, known as the Ramsey Mart, not unlike the scene in many an English market town. The same shrewd, weatherbeaten sort of faces gather round the barriers forming the bullring, as the beasts are herded through the weighing machine and into the arena.

It is a very versatile audience who gather weekly beneath that roof, where each man's daily routine is very likely to vary from animal welfare to diesel engine maintenance, from building to book-keeping and whose thoughts are more of soil analysis, and food conversion ratios than such niceties as tea-breaks, regular hours, demarkation lines and index linked pension schemes but, no matter how experienced and how devoted he may be to farming, it is very possible that the extent of benefit he may gain from many months of labour is determined by the nod of a head and the fall of the auctioneer's hammer, whether he be buying in or selling off.

Immediately the last of the animals is out of the premises a concentrated cleaning operation gets under way. All the muck and straw is swept out and the pens and stalls completely hosed down in readiness for the furniture sale of later in the week.

These furniture auctions flourish from the sad but inevitable cycle whereby, the folks who make their way over to the Isle of Man for retirement bring with them their most precious possessions such as paintings, books, silver, fine pieces of antique furniture and so on.

Though all such people are hoping to live happily for ever and ever, sooner or later these treasures of a lifetime fall to the next of kin or other beneficiaries who probably live in England, or maybe much further afield, and wish only the simplest and speediest method by which such items may be turned into cash.

The turnover of good quality items is therefore very high for the size of the population and as an estate agent might even make a commissioned sale on the same property, three times within a decade, its not such an ill wind.

Anyhow, Fay and I had been taking advantage of the situation and by the time that Ballaneddin was ready for us to move into we had acquired some very good furniture bargains.

Some pieces we had bought were very solid, heavily carved dark oak items, not bought because they were fashionable or anything like that, no, simply because they were our own particular choice, we both admired the craftsmanship, knew such detail would be too time consuming to ever be produced again and, that we both considered they would look just right, within the setting of our farmhouse home. The fact that we suddenly come into an era when everybody seemed to wish to collect almost anything that was old, and our purchases rocketed in value, was an unexpected bonus.

Many weeks the cattle stalls had been piled high with old tables, chairs, wash stands, old wireless sets, bedsteads and so on and the auctioneer had been glad to get an offer of even a pound on condition that the buyer would clear the whole lot away before next Monday's livestock Mart.

If only I could have foreseen the demand for Victoriana and the rate of inflation, then crammed some of my outbuildings full of absolute junk of the time, to bring out ten years later as a very profitable investment . . . !

With furniture in position, carpets laid and curtains hanging one could no longer tramp in and out with muddy wellingtons. I arranged for lorry loads of pebbles, fifty tons in all, to be delivered from the beach and spread across the quagmire at the front door and a layer of concrete at the rear to form a patio between the backdoor and the nearest outbuildings.

The ban on incoming livestock had been lifted and Twiggy the bulldog, together with her friend the Manx cat, that had originally come from a chip-shop in Ramsey before being taken to Cheshire, had both settled into their new surroundings quite contentedly.

Tony however, now a toddling two year old, certainly caused us some very worrying times, he had an incredible ability to completely disappear within a couple of minutes.

You'd think he was happily playing in the kitchen then I'd hear Fay shout, "Denys, he's gone!"

This was my signal to drop everything and search all round the farm yard, in and out of every outbuilding and pigsty, up and down the hedgerows and all around the long grass. We called his name again and again but knew he wouldn't reply, he was a walker, but not yet a talker. Then we might see the movement of his brightly coloured outfit right across a field, he'd found a way through one hedge and was now contemplating the next. On one occasion his poor mother was nearly hysterical, dusk had fallen, we'd already had a farmer's wife galloping all round the lanes and through the village on horseback looking for him, and it was almost pitch dark before Fay's little baby escapee was captured and brought home again.

Twiggy was very tolerant, they toddled around together and perhaps she actually enjoyed the veritable dog's life he gave her. They were both missing together one day and, after running frantically around searching in all the usual places, we noticed that in a nearby field all the cattle were grouped together where something obviously aroused their particular interest.

I approached very slowly and quietly and, sure enough, there on the grass in the centre of a circle of inquisitive Friesians sat one baby boy and his bulldog.

Obviously, out-of-reach fastenings had to be fitted to doorways to contain the junior adventurer but we were so very pleased to see him enjoying a healthy open air babyhood.

An amusing outcome of our Tony's expeditions was when I got down stairs at seven o'clock one morning to find that the bottom half of the stable-type kitchen door was wide open, and rushed upstairs again to find his cot was empty. Fortunately the crisis was cut short by the ring of the telephone.

"There was a noise at our door this morning, so we let in a cold young fellow wearing pyjamas and little red wellies", said a nearby farmer's voice, "he's in our bed at the moment, warming up."

CHAPTER 6

THE FIRST-BORN

THE basic restoration of the house was now complete, although I would still be expected to carry out more and more refinements whenever time permitted. The most beneficial of the finishing touches was concerned with heat conservation, by simply renewing those dusty, crumbling old roller blinds that we so scornfully ripped down from the window frames and burnt a few months previously. I'm sure the closely fitting blinds of years gone by were just as efficient as the fashionable and more expensive double glazing of today.

Now I needed to seriously survey the farming potential, Ballaneddin had known a very prosperous reputation, and villagers whose childhood memories went back half a century were pleased to recall their daily visits with milk cans to the dairy, the cobbled floor of the shippen all brushed out, the horses well cared for and all the agricultural equipment cleaned down at the end of the day.

Those very same horsedrawn implements were still lying around the property. There were ploughs, cultivators, hand-forged sets of harrows, two heavy stone-made land rollers and a

ridger, all the equipment to turn the soil and to not only render it down to the fine tilth required for the sowing of crops but also to carry out the laborious task of keeping the area weed-free, long before the advent of selective killers. There was a swath turner, a sweep for hay and even a horse-drawn reaper and binder, the forerunner of today's combine harvester, each item a veritable museum piece, having long outlasted its useful purpose.

The outbuildings were in various states of disrepair, maybe the woodworms were all holding hands to keep the slates up. Inside, there was a turnip slicer, a machine for chopping straw and a butter churn, all dated from days when people would stand for hours monotonously turning handles. Behind the barn there had at one time been a horse-driven mill, a system of bevelled gears that transferred the round and round activity of the horse outside, through an opening in the stonework to the grinding stones within.

There was a large assortment of horse-shoes, cast iron cog-wheels, broken hand-tools and wrought iron pieces that would have long ago been collected and re-cycled in other countries, but, on the Island the activities of a scrap metal merchant are very restricted by the cost of making shipments overseas, already the disposal of derelict cars is said to be a problem.

In its flourishing days the farm had incorporated a far larger acreage than now, but all the good arable land had been sold off to more active neighbours. Though I was so pleased to have the satisfaction of the ownership of thirty acres, I knew from the start that most of it was almost inaccessible up the hillside and regarded as virtually valueless by the local community.

Fay and I both fully realised that, from an agricultural point of view, our purchase could not become a commercial proposition. However, we had already created a very comfortable home and it was now our intention to live happily and healthily upon as much home produced food as possible, we would grow vegetables in the garden and would keep small numbers of livestock just sufficient to supply us with fresh eggs, milk and meat, but at the moment the hillside could only be regarded as a source of timber for the fire.

There is considerable prestige attached to the ownership of a farm on the Island, which we enjoyed indeed, but realised that our activities were to be on a rather Toytown scale.

We went to the Mart and came home with three ducks and a drake inside a sack and this became the first of the many hilarious happenings in our backs-to-the-land campaign. I took them to a building, shut the door behind me, opened the sack, put down food and water and left them there, huddled in a corner for the night. Next morning, I opened the door and they all flew away, like four homing pigeons. I wonder if they were put through the Mart again the following week?

Next we bought an "in-kid" goat, looking like a bag of bones standing on sticks, a pop belly and big horns, not much pedigree and not much money. (The Billy she'd been running with was available for free if we'd wanted him.)

A goat can consume and gain nourishment from a much wider range of plant life than other animals and will actually be more healthy living upon a general selection of weeds, brambles, young thistles, nettles and gorse than if restricted to a basic diet of grass only.

There was certainly an ample supply of herbage immediately available for our newcomer and she quickly set about clearing the overgrown paddock with her complicated digestive cycle. This commences first of all with a large intake of both leafy and woody fodder, which is swallowed down into number one stomach. Then comes a quiet lying down period of contentedly regurgitating and further chewing to break down the fibrous mixture for blending with the liquid in the second stomach. The next process is the chewing of "the cud"; this rises in the form of small pellets of food mixture for still more chewing and chewing. I haven't spent my time studying this action in great detail but I have read somewhere that each cud pellet is chewed for about seventy times before being dropped into stomach number three and finally number four.

This may be very interesting, and indeed a rather wonderful process, but the knowledge gave me no consolation whatsoever when, a couple of years later, I was to find that the wretched goats had chewed away all the electrical insulation off my tractor.

Usually a goat will regard any form of hedge, wall, fence or restrictive barrier as an irrisistible challenge, to be either eaten through or jumped over, but this old nanny was so far pregnant she had no immediate globetrotting ambition. Soon, her udders were swelling with milk and there were other signs that the birth was imminent.

I laid down a bed of fresh straw on the cobblestoned stable floor, with a bucket of clean water nearby but left the door open for her to exercise as she pleased.

Next morning I went in to see her proudly standing there feeding her little baby, maybe only a few minutes old. Any little creature newly coming to life is certainly a wondrous sight to see. A little goat will slide from its mother's body, give a faint cough, shake its head and try to stand up straightaway. Mother will sniff her offspring, lick it all over, removing the mucous from its nose and mouth, then it will bleat and by some marvellous instinct of nature it will make its own way round to where the mother's rich warm milk is waiting to be taken.

Unfortunately, when looking round the straw, I found the body of another less fortunate little innocent, for whom the miracle of birth had not quite worked out. However, it was lambing time, which brings its unfortunate casualties and it is not uncommon for shepherds to juggle around their orphan lambs to foster mothers. We visited a friend who had a "meg lamb" left over, a little odd man out who had no teat to go to.

"Would you like to try rearing it on your goat?" he said. Fay's maternal instinct could only allow one answer, so soon we were speeding home with a weak little newly born lamb in the car.

The hand rearing of meg lambs is regarded by some farmers as a waste of time for, no matter how much care and attention is given, so many of them never seem to gain much headway. Their most important start in life is to get the initial "biestings", the first milk from their mother while the antibodies in the colostrum are present. It has a more creamy consistency than normal milk, containing a high proportion of protein and many vital disease immunizing factors which are passed from mother to child.

Back in our stable the nanny had an ample supply to bring up two kids, but she certainly didn't want to share any whatsoever with an orphan lamb. Each time Fay held the youngest anywhere near there was an aggressive thrust with those big horns.

The mother's recognition is almost entirely by smell, so, we gently rubbed kid and lamb together to cause confusion but this made no difference. Then I remembered that, some years ago, I had been able to switch some little piglets around by pouring some cod liver oil over them.

The old goat however still loved her fishy smelling kid but just couldn't stand the sight of the horribly oily lamb. We even used the afterbirth, but still without success so now, only one alternative remained. I retrieved the dead carcase that had been removed that morning, skinned it and then pulled a crude sort of goatskin jacket over the little stranger. It looked grotesque, a rather pathetic looking sheep-in-goats-clothing.

The nanny hestitated at first and then gave the poor thing the benefit of the doubt. It was soon sucking eagerly away at her udder and a little life had been saved.

CHAPTER 7

GAINING GROUND

BEHIND the house, the land leading towards the hillside grew some gnarled old fruit trees, unpruned for many years, a few still upright but others had crashed to the ground either through age and decay or by the sheer top-weight of their uncontrolled foliage that had given way to the blustering wind.

Over many seasons dozens of cherries had fallen to the ground and the stones taken root where they lay, but by now, as the cherry saplings reached towards the sunshine, the ground at their base had developed into several almost unpenetrable thickets of dense brambles.

First attempts at burning these away proved unsuccessful for, although the dry dead grasses and leaves would blaze quite quickly there was not the sustained heat required to light the more solid vegetation, each fire would die out but still leave behind a formidable mass of barbed entanglements.

To reclaim my little jungle territory the whole lot would need to be cut down piece by piece and the springy mass collected together, compressed into more compact bonfires, and set alight with a few splashes of parafin.

So, with a small sharp axe, some long handled secateurs and a pitch-fork, the task of cutting, dragging, flattening and burning the wretched brambles began. The backs of my hands were soon torn and bleeding before I acknowledged the fact that the most sensible thing to do was to go back to the house and get an old pair of leather gloves. Other vulnerable spots were immediately behind the knees, for time and again I would take a step backwards to find my legs ensnared by thorns in the tenderness that lies just beyond the protection given at the tops of wellington boots.

Several days of concentrated effort on this rough but rewarding activity and I had gained a reasonable patch of charred paddock and salavaged a quantity of firewood. The whole area was still overhshadowed however, by a dozen or so huge trees, restricting sunlight right across my proposed vegetable area.

Magnificent specimens though they were, of chestnut, oak, beech and ash, up to eight feet in circumference, their size needed considerable reduction, no limbing had taken place for many a year and the timber so made available would be very welcome indeed.

I carried the two sections of my extending ladder to the base of a massive chestnut to investigate the possibility of removing the first of the huge branches.

I'd not yet purchased a chain saw, or ever handled one but looking upwards from the ground the job was to be very straightforward, I already knew when lopping branches off trees, one must first of all make an "undercut", otherwise, when cutting from above, the weight of the limb itself will cause a split which might easily tear downwards, taking away a damaging portion from the actual trunk.

When I'd climbed up twenty rungs or more of the ladder however, the procedure did not seem quite so simple. Especially as the top of the ladder had only just managed to reach the very branch through which I intended to saw.

Eventually I achieved a precarious position sitting astride the branch and looking dubiously down onto the delicately poised tips of the ladder below. The portion of the tree was very wide and solid, like a straddling a horse, but, with my back against the trunk, there came the sickening thought of what it would be like up there when all that hefty section of timber before me was lying on the ground and I was facing an empty space?

Where would I put my hands?

How would I hold onto a heavy chainsaw without falling forward?

Several of the limbs scheduled to be cut away probably weighed a ton. If any one of them had so much as touched the ladder my means of safe descent would have been snapped like a twig, and a further thought was whether the tree might give an upward judder when relieved of its weighty burden, sufficient to dislodge me from my lofty perch?

This ride-a-cock-horse, or rock-a-bye-baby situation was not very amusing, particularly as there was still the problem to consider of starting up the petrol motor of the saw as it stood on the ground, then hoisting the activated machine up into the air on the end of a rope.

They say that falling from a tree doesn't hurt anyone, but that nasty stop when you reach the bottom can be troublesome, especially if you happen to be carrying a roaring chain saw with you at the time.

Climbing gingerly down again from my perch I was aware of how tightly my hands were gripping each wooden rung of the ladder and the great feeling of relief when my feet finally touched the earth.

The very thought of tackling the job myself had made me scared and the realisation was rather disturbing for, I had actually spent four years of my earlier rather varied lifetime running up and down ladders as a full-time professional fire-fighter.

Maybe it was a question of discipline. It was vastly different to be in uniform as a member of a highly trained squad that spent day after day practising lifesaving routines, using first-class equipment and split-second timing. Today, there was nobody to be rescued, in fact the sole person in danger was myself, so if I didn't want to go up and cut those branches down, why the hell should I?

Back inside the house I had a cup of coffee and then phoned a firm of tree-fellers. I gave an indication of the amount of work involved and received a reply "Righto, we'll be along on Monday, weather permitting, it should only take a day".

Every man to his trade I suppose, no longer could I try to take everything in my stride, years were going by and I was now in the Isle of Man concentrating on a healthy, easy going, trouble-free way of life, more hectic days were long behind me.

Sure enough, the experts arrived as promised and by the end of the day great masses of foliage lay all across the paddock and the whole area seemed much larger and lighter with the clear sky above. I'd only asked for the limbs to be dropped to the ground and I myself would reduce it all to firewood size. I remember one of the workmen suggesting that I get it all cut up before it went hard and I really didn't undertand whether this was a piece of advice or just a sense of humour. However, about four years later when I tackled a particularly large baulk of oak that had been left uncut I was sadly to appreciate his wisdom as I sharpened and re-sharpened the teeth of my saw.

CHAPTER 8

THE FOOD FACTORY

Within the reconstituted home that had received by far the greatest amount of careful forethought and ultimate expenditure, was undoubtedly the kitchen.

What had initially been a large square dairy, cold and damp, with bare whitewashed walls and stone flagged floor, had been successfully transformed into a clean, well lit and ventilated domestic workshop, designed specifically for the preparation of all manner of health maintaining victuals.

A range of self-assembly units gave extensive work-top surfaces, at the back of which ran an electrical ring main offering the convenience of no less than ten power sockets, ready to activate a range of equipment that would boil, mix, roast, toast, grind, percolate or mince the vast variety of nutriments encountered in the culinary arts.

The floor had been given a levelling depth of concrete and an inch or so of bitumastic which, in turn, was now concealed by symmetrically laid black and white tiling.

Two large windows, looking out upon the hillside, were now in position, with very deep sills set into the thickness of the centuries-old walls fully tiled and displaying just sufficient fresh looking indoor plants to convey an atmosphere of feminine charm rather than a possible clinical, antiseptic impression of catering efficiency.

This layout might appear to be rather elaborate but it was precisely to meet our own requirements. Fay and I both had healthy appetites, both enjoyed the preparation and presentation of gourmet meals, and our ideas for future enjoyment were to include many evenings in the wining and dining of good friends, within the comfort of our home, utilising food supplies produced upon our own territory.

So, this kitchen was not designed simply for the speedy preparation of a few snacks and the modern so-called convenience foods. No, we were striving to establish the absolute extreme, which would duly incorporate the butchering of our own livestock, carrying out food preservation in the form of bottling, canning, pickling, salting, drying and even the production of home-made salamis and spaghetti. Plus, of course, the baking of bread, brewing of beer and the creation of cheeses, jams, wines, chutneys etc.

We were now fully engaged in a practical "putting the clock back" exercise, albeit a quartz electric three-hundred-and-sixty-five-day model. The initial expenditure had been heavy, but, from now onwards all those expensive commercial packages of food, so widely accepted and so extensively advertised, would gradually disappear from our domestic budget entirely.

A doorway from the kitchen led under the stairway and into an area where, in earlier times, poultry had been housed and had scratched their dust baths into an earthen floor.

Now it had become our pantry, in which stood a large deep freeze cabinet, a refrigerator and a complete wall of shelving, most of which was occupied by dozens of large glass sweet-shop jars, containing rice, lentils, beans, currents, raisins, nuts and all the other dried foods one could think of, each stored in a clean airtight condition and yet quite clearly visible. On the floor stood earthenware crocks full of flour, oatmeal and suchlike purchased direct from the Laxey Glen Mill, while, nearby stood gallon cans of cooking oil, a bin that would hold a complete sack of sugar and, in a most handy position, the inevitable keg of home brewed beer.

Outside the back door, across the yard, was yet another storage building. This had been the original cold-room, insulated to contain the dairy products long before the advent of the first refrigerator but now ideally suited for dumping vegetables and stock-piling homemade wines.

We soon became aware that, from an economic point of view, our foremost source of household heat needed to come from the timber standing on our hillside and in the near future a long term investment was required to be made in a wood burning stove that would not only cook our meals but supply also the hot domestic water and even reduce the oil consumption of the central heating arrangement. A further bonus came to mind with the thought of delicious French casseroles, with wine and herbs, simmering away in the oven for hour after hour at virtually no extra cost.

Fay certainly had quite a selection of cookery books, ranging from the days of Mrs. Beeton's best sellers right up to present day variations but I think great pleasure can be derived by not just carrying out someone else's instruction to the letter, instead, to take advantage of well known basic principles and the ideas of experts from other countries, then to venture forward with one's own interpretation incorporating certain improvisations and modifications.

In the course of time I had become the sole member of our marital partnership to carry out any of the essential unpleasant tries such as killing, plucking, skinning, gutting and cleaning, though, in fairness to Fay, I must admit that she had become quite proficient at the dismembering and subsequent dressing of crabs.

One day she was given a rather bulky plastic carrier bag, which she promptly handed over to me with her ladylike cunning that skilfully concealed any outright indication of a word of command,

"Here you are Love, you are so very good at this sort of job."

Groping inside I gingerly withdrew quite a smelly feathered assortment. There was mallard, half a dozen teal ducks, four woodpigeons and a further four woodcock, all of which had been shot the previous evening.

Really, they should have been hanging legs downwards overnight, with air circulating while they lost their bodyheat, but as the weather was quite chilly I was not too perturbed. This hanging procedure is to add flavour, make the meat more tender and cause the feathers to come away more easily. The number of days in suspense is varied according to the species, its estimated age and of course to the palate of the individual who is expected to devour the end product.

I like my own meat to have flavour, but, by no means must it approach the mild putrification that other people's stomachs claim to relish, and I was quite sure that one night spent within the confines of a plastic bag would be an ample length of time.

Plucking birds is mainly just a matter of patience, especially if you have several to deal with, generally you just tug sharply at little tufts in the opposite direction in which they are naturally lying, but over-enthusiasm will tear the skin and spoil the appearance for the final presentation, unless of course, you hide your mistake by doing a neat surgical repair with needle and cotton. The larger wing feathers require a little more effort but if you happen to become involved with a real tough old-timer, a kettle of boiling water poured over will ease the situation, but this makes the corpse messy and the kitchen smelly.

The next part of preparation is called "drawing", which means opening up a hole in the unfortunate creature's back-end with a pair of scissors, poking your fingers inside and drawing out everything that's loose. From the messy cluster of slippery entrails you can, if you so wish, salvage the giblets, which consist of the gizzard — being a little bag of muscle full of tiny stones and partially broken down food — the heart and the liver, taking care to cut away its sack of very bitter green liquid gall without causing a puncture.

Then you wipe the carcase as clean as possible, inside and out with a damp cloth. At this stage the thing looks a bit untidy so you smarten it up by twisting both wings behind into a sort of double-Nelson. The skin that was once around the neck you push out of sight into the front end and tie both legs together to conceal the jagged hole your fingers made at the rear.

You then stand back to admire your handiwork, and, now that its dry you notice there are hairs sticking out of its chest which you forgot to singe off earlier in the wretched proceedings.

Anyhow, the job was duly completed, sink all washed out, everywhere tidy and a neat line of birds were displayed across the kitchen table awaiting Fay's critical inspection prior to being popped inside the fridge for future enjoyment.

Really, the woodpigeons are so plentiful on the Island that they are a menace and rather than go through the unsavoury rigmaroll just mentioned it is far quicker to simply peel off the skin from the plump little breasts and cut away the meat with a small sharp knife.

The original plastic carrier had contained four woodcock which had now been plucked, drawn and cleaned out, but this is a much-prized little wild bird which is traditionally served upon the gourmet's table roasted, with its entrails still within and eaten in its entirety. This however was just not my idea of a delicacy, and bearing in mind all the attention that had been devoted to kitchen hygiene, and considering the rotten smells encountered when pulling out the bowels of any dead creature, I cannot understand why anyone should want to eat bird-muck with a knife and fork, no matter how delicately prepared and how tastefully seasoned.

CHAPTER 9

SOLID SALLY

WE placed a simple advert in the local newspaper reading . . . "WANTED. Solid fuel cooker . . ." followed by our phone number, knowing that ample supplies of timber and peat were freely available, the only expense being the actual manual and mechanical work of sawing, chopping, digging and transportation.

Many glossy brochures bore attractive illustrations of cookers and boilers which were claimed to run very economically on a variety of solid fuels. We'd been in and out of showrooms examining some superb models, ideally suited for installation in the newly created kitchen, unfortunately, each price ticket we read brought about a firm reluctance to expend that amount of capital, hence the decision to advertise, the cost had been minimal so now we waited for the response, if any.

Surprise, surprise, the phone rang and a male voice spoke of a cooker with a trade name that we'd never heard of but with an asking price that sounded extremely acceptable.

"How old is it?" was the obvious question.

"Brand new, never been used", came the response.

We were both far too experienced to believe that some Manx fairy would pick up the phone and offer us a bargain, just like that. No, there must obviously be a snag somewhere, maybe a complete misunderstanding, perhaps we were being offered some item of camping equipment. There was only one way to find out, for we couldn't simply dismiss the possibility as being highly improbable. An explanation was still needed, so we went along to the address that had been given.

A tall elderly gentleman led us to his garage, swung back the door and there, standing at the rear of the building, was a very solid looking cast iron cooking stove. Just what we wanted!

Inside the oven the loosely fitted metal shelves were still wrapped in the manufacturers greased paper, the yellow fire bricks fitted round the interior of the hearth were clean and unscorched, the edges of the bars forming the grate bottom were sharp and clean just as they had left the iron foundry. That stove had certainly never been in use.

The owner explained that he had come to that house six years previously, when he had retired from farming, and the intention had been to have the stove fitted, but, due to some change of plan, it had stood in the garage ever since. This of course gave a very reasonable and acceptable explanation for a "new" cooker to be offered so much less in price than anything else we had seen, and it certainly looked ideal for our purpose.

Firstly a few doubtful thoughts had to be overcome, was it absolutely complete, or would bits and pieces be needed before the boiler could be connected to the water supply? Another thought that passed through my mind was that it looked rather plain and basically functional, whereas the showroom models were offered in a range of pastel shades, had stainless steel hotplates and incorporated various chromium plated fittings. Anyhow we had a little haggle, reached a mutual figure and I paid on the spot.

Estimating that the whole contraption would weigh about three hundredweight I decided to make another visit, with a couple of volunteers to help me slide it up some wooden planks into a van, in the meantime all removable parts were taken away in the car.

A few days later it had been successfully collected, and brought home to be carefully eased along the hallway on rollers into its pre-agreed position in the kitchen. Inside the oven was a pamphlet giving general instructions, but the very nature of the typesetting of the plain black and white publication gave the impression that it was certainly more than six years old. When a plumber came along he not only confirmed to our satisfaction that all the necessary fittings were intact but when questioned about its possible vintage he said "I've certainly not seen a model like this in my lifetime".

I'm sure the farmer had been delighted with the transaction, but so too were we, we'd have bought it if it had been described as twenty-six or even thirty-six years old.

Obtaining some lengths of cast iron piping of the correct diameter to fit the chimney, I cut a round hole in the kitchen roof and in due course we were able to stand back and admire our "Solid

Sally" cooker firmly in position, with her upright stovepipe appearing not very unlike Stephenson's Rocket, all ready for ignition and the build-up of a head of steam.

Shortly before this time, a terrific gale had swept the Island one night and I stepped out of the house into the peace and sunshine of the following morning to find a lofty pine tree had crashed down and its tip was only a yard or so from the kitchen window.

Where the base of the trunk had been embedded for so many years, a large circle of pasture, soil and roots now stood erect like some ungainly cart-wheel at the end of a long disconnected axle, the thick roots extending from either side having been twisted over with the fury of the wind and sheer weight of the mighty evergreen.

"Sheila's husband is coming along at the weekend, to attend to the pine tree", announced my wife, coming off the phone with a smugness of having organised something while I was still thinking about it. At that time I did not even know who Sheila was, but since arriving on the Island as a stranger, Fay had certainly been made very welcome and new friendships had been developing easily. At the weekend I was to learn that my visitor was a very experienced woodsman whose craft covered a range that extended from the felling of timber, right through to the creation of some quite remarkable surealistic wood carvings.

A man of very few words, he came round the side of the house, looked at the crumpled mass of prostrate foliage, then turned on his heel to bring a petrol-driven chain saw from the back of his Landrover.

This was already the second occasion upon which a kindly neighbour had brought a chain saw into action at Ballaneddin, sooner or later it was bound to become necessary to purchase one of those highly effective, but horribly dangerous items of machinery for, having made an all-out effort in the successful creation of an ideal country dwelling, my next priorities must be the joint production of fuel and food and the ill-wind of earlier that week had already dumped a ton of pinewood, almost onto my doorstep.

Eager to learn, I watched with interest as the expert poured a petrol/oil mixture into the fuel tank and then, with the machine standing on the ground, he put his left foot firmly through the handle to give stability, then gave a couple of sharp, fully choked wrenches on the starter cord which brought the little engine to life with a harsh, staccato, unsilenced bark. It was certainly no toything for the amateur handyman.

The cutting chain itself is propelled via a centrifugal clutch, whereby it remains stationery while the engine is only set at its tick-over speed, but immediately the slightest pressure is brought onto the operating trigger, a bicycle chain armed with a razor-blade on every link rotates at a horrifying speed, able to tear ferociously into anything unfortunate enough to be within its reach.

Obviously the operator must always wear close fitting clothing, the consequences of a sleeve or scarf being caught up within the teeth of that whirling chain are unbearable and the ideal working position is to be within strong steel capped boots, on firm, level ground.

The immediate programme was to cut away all the protruding branches and then to slice the entire tree trunk into rings, like large dartboards about a foot thick, which could be later split into blocks of acceptable size for our "new" cooking stove.

The ground was by no means ideal, it was uneven, slippery with wet grass and littered with splintered debris. As the smaller timbers were sawn away to gain access to the trunk I dragged them away from under my companion's feet, 'til eventually he was able to gain clear contact with the principal limbs and take them off at a point close to the trunk. Those that had been growing nearest to the ground of this enormous Christmas tree were, of course, the thickest, but, with a few seconds burst of the furious little petrol engine were completely severed. My new friend stepped confidently over the trunk, repeating this treatment from side to side and I was delighted to see that with each squeeze of the throttle trigger more and more firewood was becoming available.

The forestry man trimmed off the final branch and stepped back. Suddenly, to our absolute amazement, the whole naked trunk made a slight upward movement, increasing with speed until that huge wheel-shaped concentration of soil encrusted roots thumped back into position, bringing a ragged looking Totem pole starkly upright. Having been flattened by the storm and held down by the weight of its own branches this

restriction had now been released and the trunk had regained the vertical position by the elasticity of its distorted roots.

We looked up at the grotesque pole, and each gave a rather silly laugh, both knowing what a terrible accident there could easily have been. Forestry work is recognised for its dangers, the felling of large trees being particularly hazardous, but the thought of being injured by a tree that jumped upright seemed so ridiculous that we adjourned to the kitchen for cups of coffee and to quietly think about it.

Eventually the old pine tree was lain low for a second time and duly reduced to suitably sized portions of firewood. Fay was very pleased when I lit the old Solid Sally cooker. The top-plate became hot quite quickly, so did the water pipes round the back, and within a short space of time, and the use of a couple of armfuls of pinewood logs, we had a boiling kettle and a domestic cylinder full of piping hot water.

The faint rustic aroma of smouldering timber blended perfectly with the farmhouse setting and home-made bread was promised for the near future. Everything had worked out to our absolute satisfaction, the purchase of the stove, its transportation, the plumbing, the fitting of the chimney and now the readiness of a whole pile of good fuel, we were quite proud of the advancement made.

That particular day was to be completed by taking a run in the car, then returning in the evening to enjoy one of Fay's exquisite meals by candle-light in the comfort of our old world dining room, a bottle of good wine, a hot bath and an early night. What more could one wish for?

The stove was stoked to the top with blocks of wood, the damper closed down so that there would be a mass of glowing embers for our return, and away we went.

The early evening was enjoyed thoroughly, aided by the satisfaction of the day and the anticipation of the evening's proposed activities. But I was blissfully unware that the wind direction had changed back home at Ballaneddin. Soon I was to learn a couple of very elementary rules of countrylife, in the harshest way.

Firstly, you must never ever put green wood (straight from a living tree) into a cooking stove, especially any of the pine varieties and secondly, when you've fitted your stove, don't go out and leave it burning unless you've fitted an appropriate type of cowl on the top of your chimney, that will satisfactorily deflect the wind from any direction.

"HELL HATH NO FURY, LIKE A WOMAN WHO COMES HOME TO FIND HER BRAND NEW KITCHEN FULL OF ACRID SMOKE AND SOOT!"

CHAPTER 10

FUEL

WE had both been completely carried away with our enthusiasm for the bargain-priced old cooker and to find the kitchen full of smoke certainly jolted us back to reality. The first and most important matter was to establish what building regulations were applicable when one poked an iron stove pipe through a timbered ceiling. These government requirements can so often seem to be too involved, expensive and time consuming but of course it is the householder's safety and welfare that is so very much in mind.

The buildings and the nearby trees were much higher than the outlet point of the pipe, consequently there was a great deal of turbulence. No matter which direction the wind was blowing there was nearly always a terrible backdraught. I added a further length of pipe to gain height, then another, and then began a trial and error period back and forth to a builders' merchant for a satisfactory type of cowling. One style was designed to spin round and round in the wind, another would swing into wind by means of a rudder but I eventually settled for a rigid "H"-shaped fitting which seemed best for my particular set of circumstances.

The chimney, carrying hot smoke and gases, only travelled for a few feet inside the kitchen before going out through the roof into the fresh air. This caused a further complication, for condensation was taking place and oozing right down the inside of the iron pipe, into the stove itself, in the form of filthy black tarry acid. This meant that the lengths of pipe I'd fitted outside the building had to be replaced by some expensive insulated tubing. More or less one chimney inside another with about half an inch thickness of non-combustible material in between the two.

Eventually I got it right, smoke went up the chimney, and no trickles of rain water or acid came down. The cooker itself was no trouble whatsoever, being quite simply an iron box to burn wood in, with an opening to control its air intake, an oven at the side and a tray beneath to take away the ash, which would still have value with the compost and manure in the garden. All that we needed now was an unlimited supply of good dry hardwood.

On the hillside there were several acres of woodland and making a tour of my recently acquired estate, I struggled through the dense entanglement of brambles amongst the gorse and heather, noticing that large trees had been felled within the last fifty years and from their stumps had sprung a multitude of saplings. Perhaps this area of land, too steep for cultivation, had, over a long period of time been controlled and utilised as a coppice, certainly this procedure had been of great benefit in England over many centuries, whereby large trees were felled for general timber purposes and the subsequent growth that came from the stumps became a crop of handy sized firewood logs every dozen years or so. A far seeing family would ensure a rotation was created whereby the coppice would keep the home fires burning for future generations.

Timber for fuel must have been much more important to the earlier inhabitants of Ballaneddin, for there is no coal mined upon the Island whatsoever, and the only alternative was to dig the peat. I was concerning myself with the burning of timber purely because the other fuels, although so readily available, were becoming more and more expensive. Consequently, when a friend suggested that we should work a peat "claim" together I was delighted.

The most productive peat areas are under Government control. No charge was made at that time, but every person who goes digging is under obligation to carry out certain simple regulations, such as the requirement that you keep solely to the numbered plot that has been made available to you, that you leave the area tidy at the finish of your excavation, and place some surface turf back in position. This privilege is granted to any private individual who wishes to augment his domestic fuel requirements, but no commercial operation is allowed.

Our allocated plot was in an area off the mountain road known as "Penny Pot", about four miles from home. There we parked the car at the roadside and began to climb up the hill, which was littered with wooden stakes bearing numbers. There might be some first come, first served, form of distribution, or maybe it was the people who had been regular peat diggers over the years, who got the most convenient sites near to the roadside. Anyhow, we trudged up the steep slippery slope with our spades across our shoulders until we found the appropriate number.

Several people were already hard at work, for digging is only permitted between certain dates of the year. We saw that, having taken off the top sods and placed them nearby for subsequent re-laying, the basic labour involved the cutting out of wet blocks of heavy black claylike substance and endeavouring to stack them in a sort of wall-full-of-holes formation so that the mountain wind could dry them out. Looking round the site I could see there were blocks being dug in all shapes and sizes and a variety of precarious looking drying walls under construction, but it was very noticeable that the more experienced prospectors had brought with them lengths of timber, corrugated metal sheets and suchlike, to ensure their weighty nuggets were placed upon a reasonably dry and level base.

The more peat you extracted, the more black water trickled into the little quarry you were creating, and the deeper you got, the greater was the lift required by each piece you cut and heaved out on the spade. By the end of the digging season we were standing up to our ankles in slippery peat juice and heaving up the slices to above our shoulder level.

Some while later we both went along in my old 15 cwt van and in theory we should have found our blocks all dried out and firm. But our little drying walls had been either pushed over by the sheep, blown over by the wind, or maybe just poorly built in the first place, anyhow, most of the stuff was lying on the ground, still quite wet. We started putting it piece by piece into sacks and then picking our way carefully down the slope, stepping over little streamlets and zig-zagging around other people's excavations till we reached the roadway. Climbing back up the hill again each time with an empty sack was even more tiring than making one's way down again. On a later occasion we took along a lightweight roly-poly wheelbarrow, of a modern design which had a big plastic football in front instead of a wheel. It bounced downhill alright with about a hundredweight each time, but still had to be carried back up to the top again.

Unfortunately, half the weight that we were carrying consisted of water and when my share had dried out in a few weeks of sunshine at home, each piece had shrivelled down to less than half its original size. It was now quite hard, clean to handle and was very satisfactory to burn in either Solid Sally or the open fire, but when

I looked at the puny little stack, that had taken so many energetic man-hours, so much petrol and so much expenditure on the quenching of digger's thirst each evening, I very much doubt if it had really been an economic operation.

CHAPTER 11

MORE FUEL

ALTHOUGH only seasoned, dry hardwoods were suitable for feeding into the cooking stove, the open grate in the living room would accept more-or-less anything, provided there was a good enough draught to get all the smoke up the chimney and it wasn't a sort of timber that would throw sparks out onto the carpet.

Still quite a few old beams were lying around from the house restoration so some of these pieces were used to form two "X" shapes, which, when joined together with old floor boards became a sawing horse, upon which other lengths were laid to be sawn to size. There were plenty of fallen trees and broken branches that could be dragged along and I found the activity quite satisfying, just one of the necessary facets of this healthy, back to the land life we had chosen. When sawing logs you need to work at your own speed and develop a relaxed rhythm. Your mind can be contentedly wandering over a multitude of reminiscences, as long as you keep that saw going backwards and forwards. You can think with satisfaction of the slowly growing accumulation of fuel you are creating, and, most important, banish all thoughts about that poor aching arm of yours.

Not many weeks passed before the novelty of this monotonous to and fro marathon began to fade.

"Did you really need to put that extra log on the fire Fay?" I kept asking, having found by now that the household requirements were about one hundredweight every day which consumed quite a lot of my time and energy, especially as we had no stockpile readily at hand. We certainly appreciated the wisdom of the creation of those accumulated supplies that you see stacked outside French farmhouses. Collecting a few sticks together for a weekend camp fire in the middle of summer is all part of the fun, but there's nothing funny about running out of logs for your cooking stove when it happens to be pouring with rain outside in midwinter.

The time had come to make a further onslaught upon our much diminished capital by the purchase of our own petrol driven chainsaw. The local agricultural engineer was very helpful and spent a long time giving me the benefit of his own experiences and eventually I came away with a brand new appliance, having seen it started, stopped and restarted on half a dozen occasions, seen it cleanly take off a couple of log slices at the side of the workshop and made my own tentative first few cuts. "If you have any trouble whatsoever don't hesitate to come along and see me" he had called as I drove away, and having noticed that there were no fewer than twelve saws, in various stages of repair on and around his workbench I came to the conclusion that, with a turnover like that, there must be a chain saw used on almost every farm in the north of the Island.

With any sort of machinery the correct care and maintenance is so very important, this particularly applies to the actual sawing chain where lubrication is absolutely essential. Some models have a built-in automatic oil pump which ensures a constant supply whenever the engine is running but my own was manually operated by thumb pressure on a small plunger every few seconds of cutting.

Soon after I got back home Fay and I set to work on our first power assisted log cutting. After several sympathetic warnings of "Do be very, very careful with it Denys", I started up the motor and began thumbing oil onto the cutting chain. Fay kept lifting short lengths of timber across the cuddie (that's the Scottish name for sawing horse) where I reduced them to ten inch lengths of firewood. This particular task would have been rather tedious to attempt single handed, for, every time timber was put across the cuddie or moved along as the slices were made, a person on his own would have to put the running machine down on the ground and then bend to pick it up again, making progress rather restricted.

We worked very well together as a team and within half an hour had gone through all the wood we had brought down to the side of the house. I switched off the engine and was relieved by the silence, for I had been sawing quite close to the house and workshop, consequently all the time that continual roar had been bouncing back off the stone walls onto my eardrums; our next logging session must be carried out in a more open position. Another point to be remembered for the future was to choose a day when there was not a strong wind blowing, for, as I was that much nearer to the machine than Fay, I had sawdust in my eyes, hair, nostrils, down my shoes, down my neck, everywhere. We were absolutely delighted with our new toy, but still had a lot to learn to put it to its best advantage.

That half hour's activity I had found quite tiring for, apart from the actual physical requirement of holding up the weighty unit which consisted of saw, engine and petrol tank, a very good grip with both hands was needed to control the vibration. There was also the nervous tension, the fear, knowing the saw was potentially lethal and the slightest lack of concentration could have terrible consequences.

We must have sawn through many tons of logs in the years that were to come but we made it a routine that the saw would only be running for half an hour at any one session lest either of us began to lose the combined alertness that was so essential. This coincided with the fact that by then not only would my back be aching but the petrol tank would be ready for a refill, every tooth of the chain would need a couple of strokes of the sharpening file, and the air filter would need cleaning out with the vacuum cleaner. We had very little trouble so long as the petrol/oil ratio was correct and the sparking plug was clean, this was fortunate, for, pulling without success on a starter cord can be very frustrating, and it's no use thinking you might start it with a tow along the lane.

Other tools which came into use for our fuel collection were one large felling axe, one smaller axe, one ten pound sledge hammer, a couple of wedges for splitting down the grain and a bow shaped log saw, each of which I painted red, simply because it was so much easier to find every item again when thrown down in long grass.

We now had all equipment for cutting our own timber, but cutting is only half the operation, it still needed to be transported. Every single piece had to be either carried, dragged or wheeled from where it was found, right the way to the back kitchen door. All this was good healthy exercise in the fresh air and provided no accidents took place it should have proved beneficial all round but when visitors came over in the summer and began to tell us both, "You are very lucky you know, getting your fuel for nothing, coal and heating oil are terrible prices now", I would quietly think of the petrol, the oil and the elbow grease that had been involved, but would say nothing, for this was the life of our choice, and had anyone asked Fay if she would have liked to return to life in a ladies hairdressing salon in Cheshire, they would be left with no doubts whatsoever that Ballaneddin gave her all the pleasures and satisfaction she wanted in life.

Within a mile of home was a depot of the Forestry Board where lorry loads of pinewood poles were brought in from the plantations to make into fencing posts. They were made pointed at one end simply by four short cuts on a circular saw bench, so from the production of every post — and they made many thousands — there were four wedge shaped pieces left over. These "pointings" as they were called were offered for sale to anyone who went along with their own empty sacks and transport. We used to fill several trailer loads and found them very useful. From the same depot I could get supplies of sawdust to put down with the chicken litter and from another area I would collect the outer strips of bark and wood from larger trees that could become fencing.

A little steam railway had once run through the fields, parallel with the road in front of the house but had now been closed down as non-profitmaking, the railway lines were sold off and I bought a lorry load of the wooden sleepers. These were pickled in creosote, smelt strongly and make a lot of smoke. I would have been far happier to see the old Victorian engine go puffing along the line, pulling its carriages to Ramsey, than to think I was throwing upon the fire all that remained of a more peaceful bygone era.

CHAPTER 12

SELF-SUFFICIENCY

WE were ever so happy in our new home, revelling in the tremendous satisfaction of having restored the crumbling country dwelling of yesteryear, but incorporating all those up-to-date facilities and personal refinements, to create a quite distinctive residence.

Our whole life was now so interesting and exciting, for we were reclaiming wilderness to cultivate vegetables and gradually gathering a selection of livestock around us. This was not being achieved without a few hilarious mistakes, however. Shortly after our ducks had flown away we bought some ewes from the auction, only to find when they were delivered that they were so old they'd got no teeth left.

The initial feeling of annoyance soon gave way to laughter for we could simply send them back to another auction next week, and providing there was some other mug there willing to nod his head up to our price, the only loss would be the auctioneer's fee and the transport involved, so it was not a major disaster, but no wonder they had seemed so reasonable.

The old nanny goat grazed peacefully in the paddock one day, but about an hour later I found her lying dead on the ground her belly grotesquely swollen, almost to bursting point.

Goats are quite hardy creatures really and on the few occasions that they became ill appropriate action can quickly be taken but with this particular tragedy there had been no warning whatsoever. From time to time, over the years that were to come I encountered goats that had obviously taken something poisonous. If the animal was just standing still, tail limp, head hung down with a glassy look in the eyes as though it was going to drop dead, I would straightaway run to the house, grab a package of margarine, melt it in a pan on the stove, pour it into a beer bottle, then Fay and I would run outside again and while I forced apart the animal's jaws she would pour the greasy liquid directly into its gullet. On each occasion the unfortunate creature had then shaken its head, given a few burps and within the hour had returned to normal grazing.

We had been so very thrilled to see the first baby goat to be born at Ballaneddin, but I soon realised that it was not actually a very robust specimen. In fact it was an absolute weakling and although I ensured that it had ample nourishment, and that its companion lamb did not take everything, it became a rather puny creature. Apart from its obvious physical shortcomings, it kept getting its head caught in the wire netting time and time again, so much so that we came to the conclusion that the poor little wretch also suffered some form of mental deficiency.

Anyone rearing livestock must only be concerned with absolutely healthy specimens, so, with reluctance, I had to administer to our little first-born the ultimate treatment, by inserting a small piece of lead behind its ear.

I had brought my competition rifle over from England and had registered my ownership with the Isle of Man Police but had not yet got round to joining any one of the rifle clubs that flourish on the Island. I had seen by the competition results published in the local papers that the shooting standard was very high indeed.

So, initially, our desired accumulation of livestock got off to a disappointing start. There was however an absolute exception, for a fellow gave me three bantam hens.

"They're becoming a nuisance around the garden", he said, "but I just throw them a handful of corn now and again and they go into my workshop and lay eggs inside a box of nails."

They were nice little birds, very tame and settled down quickly to their new surroundings, except that one fell in a bucket of creosote, so then there were two.

Many people enjoy feeding a few bantams, but when they start to become too numerous they're quite eager to give them away, rather than undertake a much more terminal action. Consequently, we were soon given a few more hens and a couple of cocks, and began collecting an abundance of good, fresh, home produced eggs but of course they were little over half the size of the standard egg that one can collect from any supermarket.

In the springtime all the hens wanted to go broody and hatch their youngsters, some secreted themselves away in the various buildings or hedgerows for a month and then made a very proud entrance into the farmyard with maybe a dozen tiny balls of brown fluff bobbing along behind them.

This was indeed a wonderful sight, really heartwarming, that must be fully enjoyed to the absolute maximum, for in my case there was certainly to be no satisfaction at the end of the little creature's lifecycle, I would sadly be the executioner. Later to banish all thoughts of the gruesome procedures that had passed when I sat down to enjoy my wife's savoury dishes.

The chicks that hatched out the first year were indeed a variety of colours for the two cocks were entirely different but, there was also a rather fine looking cock pheasant who had spent a lot of time with the little hens. I could have shot him many a time, had I wanted, but got more pleasure out of seeing him proudly strutting around. If I was to take aim and pull the trigger it would be as sporting as shooting a blindfolded hostage.

Obviously this bantam flock had to be kept under control in fairness to my neighbours when they were seeding the nearby fields. I don't know whether a pheasant will actually mate with a bantam, but we certainly enjoyed many a plump little carcase that had a very definite game flavour.

Fay and I loved our carefree life, together on the Isle of Man, all manner of actual work involved with the finishing touches to our home were forms of absolute pleasure. On wet days there were shelves to put up, windows sills to tile and so on, while outside I managed to carry out such refinements as a rose garden and rockery before the front door, painted and repaired a fine pair of

cart wheels that looked far better in an ornamental category in front of the house, than festooned with cobwebs in the barn.

They looked very picturesque, well, I thought so, for although at the end of the operation of reconstruction, the front of the house had taken so many tons of stone from the beach to make it look respectable, now the whitewashed buildings, the stones, the brightly painted cart wheels and a couple of decorative tubs united into a colourful but rural charm.

I was so very happy on the surface, but in the back of my mind was that rather sickly feeling that I had created a wonderful homestead but still had no income to support my family.

Fay and I were not just a couple of young misfits, who had opted out of the general way of society to do the "in-thing", "self-sufficiency", or any fashionable wordage like that. All we wanted was a peaceful and healthy existence in the land of our choice, with our baby son.

We were not exactly youngsters either, for between us we had already three adult children following their own careers across the water.

There were certainly many people over in England who were pursuing their own back-to-nature theme. Unfortunately with some, their image seemed to involve long unkempt hair and a very sparing application of soap and water, while passing a rather idle existence, accepting the weekly generosity of the welfare state.

The Manx Government offers all the usual Social Security benefits but, very wisely restricts its distribution to established Isle of Man residents only, otherwise it would be just so easy for people to come over to the Island, work in the tourist trade during the ten weeks of the summer season and then draw the dole money all through the rest of the year. Consequently, each September sees a mass exodus of these migrant workers.

Fay and I had spent the bulk of our separate working lives in successful self-employment so our move across to the Island involved not only the challenge of a tumbledown farmhouse, but also the intrigue and uncertainty of how a suitable income could be produced. Had we met a couple of decades or so younger we might have set off across the prairie lands of the Wild West in a covered wagon, although knowing full well that those pioneering days could not possibly have been so romantic as portrayed by the film studios of today.

I was delighted that my wife had settled so easily into the friendly Island community and for myself, who had spent a lifetime to and fro, and, at one time had carried out an extensive study of the Island's folk-lore and its association with unorthodox medicine, now at last I was fulfilling a long standing ambition.

Wandering around the local churchyard, reading the old tombstones, we learnt that Ballaneddin had been occupied by other Teares over the course of time, maybe not my direct relatives, but the information added interest and gave further food for meditation when sitting before the flickering fire on winter nights.

A certain anxiety was however beginning to creep into our lives, no simple means of producing a modest income had yet come to mind. Obviously, in one particular manner a most substantial profit could be made, but, we were both determined that, come what may, we must never sell our beloved homestead.

CHAPTER 13

FRESH AND FREE

NOW that the basic work had been completed we felt justified in taking occasional days purely for the purpose of thoroughly enjoying the magical enchantment of our chosen Isle.

Although just a mere dot of ink on an atlas this little country is surrounded by no less than one hundred miles of the most delightful coastal scenery anyone could wish to see.

Most of this coastline is of rugged headlands where the waves dash themselves upon the rocks far below and the seabirds gracefully carve their way through the bracing salt air, swooping down, snatching some morsel from the water to feed the hungry offspring they have hatched in nests precariously sited high upon the cliff face. The same scene that must have been gazed upon by the Viking settlers but enacted for thousands upon thousands of years even before any human ear was around to catch those strange unmusical sea calls that echo from the massive limestone chasms and caves.

Small streams make their way down from the mountainous inland, join together and widen to form delightful trout-filled rivers, tumbling their way down through leafy glens, reaching the tiny fishing ports where harbours have been built to give shelter when the merciless onslaught of the Irish Sea storms lash the Island.

Looking from the bedroom windows, through the trees, our nearest shore lay just a mile across the fields. This was the western coast of the northern portion of the Island, instead of rocky headlands there were miles of sand and pebble beaches which stretched right to the northernmost tip, where, from the lighthouse, one can look across to Scotland, whose mountains seem so tantilisingly near on a clear day, then running south down the eastern face right to the town of Ramsey. A total distance of over twenty miles of unspoilt beach where, for most of the year you will not see another person in sight.

Outside the holiday season it was interesting to come across a set of footprints in the sand and to speculate about which particular person had been there earlier that day and to try to ascertain what size of dog had been scampering alongside.

My own initial visits down to the beach were certainly not occasions for stepping briskly along at the waters edge with the wind in my hair, taking deep breaths and feeling the world was at my feet. No, on the contrary, the first excursions took the form of very restricted tortoise-like shuffles, with Fay and I trying to keep our toddling son from sitting fully clothed on the wet sand and accompanied by our slow old bulldog bitch, Twiggy, whose short, stumpy legs produced a mini-hippo gait as she snuffled and snorted along with an air of utter disgust at getting her feet wet.

Subsequent visits were to yield an interesting supply of useful driftwood, lengths of tow rope and broken nets from the trawlers that could still be of use to keep birds off the fruit trees and the vegetable garden. Occasional fishboxes, floating in on the waves were first of all made of timber but, within the space of just a few years were entirely replaced by much lighter and more easily mass-produced plastic types, which were well worthy of collection for garden use.

Around most of the Island any floating bottles would get smashed upon the rocks and be reduced once more to grains amongst the sand by the power of the sea but, on our nearby sandy beach young Tony grew up to appreciate that his pocket money could be quite pleasantly enhanced by spotting the "returnable" specimens that came ashore intact and merited a few coppers each from a friendly shopkeeper. On two instances there was the excitement of finding bottles containing messages, the first was from a young girl in Ireland who gave family details and with whom various leters were duly exchanged, and secondly from a schoolgirl in Wales whose message quite simply asked that the finder should send her a picture postcard and would receive another by return. This exchange duly took place, first having explained to Tony that I was quite sure that the expected procedure was to send the card via the local letter box, not to just stick it in the bottle and throw it back in the sea.

Plenty of foodstuffs are freely available at the water's edge and once one had learnt their exact location it was just a matter of collecting one's requirements at a time when the tide was sufficiently low.

Cockles and mussels were readily available and could be served in a very tasty selection of seafood dishes, periwinkles could be very quickly collected by the handful at any time of the year, but Fay's culinary preparation never seemed to venture beyond the time honoured routine of leaving few hours in water to cleanse themselves, five minutes in boiling water and then to gobble them down, one at a time, as fast as your pin can hook each one out of its shell. There are plenty of the older folk on the Island today who can remember setting off to school in the morning with a pocket-full of winkles, that were probably more beneficial than the multitude of sweet products available to children nowadays.

Limpets, those conical shaped shells that stick onto smooth rock surfaces in such great numbers, I understood to be edible. Fortunately Fay and I both shared that enthusiasm for tasting something different, convincing each other that if a meal is prepared from any form of meat produced from a freshly killed and healthy creature it can't be far wrong.

Down to the rocks I went, armed with penknife and plastic bucket and was soon to learn how the grip of these shells increased to a fantastic strength even as I approached. The easiest method of dislodging turned out to be by stealthily catching the largest specimens unaware, with a hefty first-time only, kick. The preparation and seasoning was all carefully carried out according to an old-time recipe book and smelled good, but the wretched little morsels of meat turned out to be so very tough that we never tried them again. As far as I was concerned they could all remain in peace at the water's edge, until such time as a shipwrecked mariner crawled ashore, especially if he happened to have a mincing machine with him.

At the time of the year when the tides were at their lowest several of my acquaintances would each set off by car to reach some particular part of the coastline where they knew, from past years of experience, good sized crabs could be found. Their only equipment was a pair of wellington boots, a piece of wood with an iron hook attached and a sack in which to bring home their captives.

Hanging up in one of the outbuildings at the farm I had come across a metal rod, about three feet long, with a handle at one end and turned over to the shape of a hook at the other. First of all I could not visualise its purpose but now, in due course, I too, when time permitted, would poke around under the boulders and between the crevices at low water.

Undaunted by the pathetic outcome of my limpet collecting expedition but still spurred on by our joint desire to sample everything that was both fresh and free, I was pleased to learn in a century-old cook book of the palatability of razor shell fish. Normally, these items of sea life are only seen as empty broken shells, like blades of the old fashioned style of cut-throat razors, amongst the debris that nature deposits along the shore at each turn of the tide.

The quest for live razor shells turned out to be one of our most hilarious of family pantomimes, for, believe it or not, to catch these lowly defenceless creatures, which have neither arms, legs, fins nor flippers, the human being needs a keen eye, the split-second reaction of an athlete, combined with the basic qualification of an enthusiastic grave digger.

The only time to make any attempt at catching razor fish has got to be at an occasion of a very low tide, preferably just before the moon decides it's time to stir everything up and send the waves all rolling in again.

Tony was by now a boisterous little fellow, absolutely revelling in the day to day excitement of our way of life and already Fay and I were looking quite eagerly forward to a few months time when a little local playschool had expressed willingness to take the responsibility off our hands for a few hours each week.

Anyhow, the three of us set off down to the water's edge wearing our habitual uniforms of anoraks and rubber knee boots, I had a garden spade under my arm and, with a certain amount of apprehension, my dear wife carried the inevitable plastic bucket.

Then we began to walk very slowly, very carefully and in absolute silence along the wet sand hand in hand, parallel to the water. A hundred yards or so at that pace and Tony became restless, his mother began to lose concentration and I had a rather foolish feeling that my leg had been well and truly pulled. "You've got to be quick, 'cause they jump", the fellow had told me in Ramsey, but that was after we'd swapped a few pints of bitter, so I now began to doubt his story.

Travelling further along Fay had to keep Tony in order. "Be very quiet, walk very softly" she whispered, "Daddy's going to catch us some fish!" Such confidence made the situation seem even more idiotic.

Then suddenly, just before our advancing feet there was a distinct "PLOP", and a slight movement in the watery sand. I quickly dug down to a depth of nearly two feet, but was far too late, I'd just missed my very first razor shell.

The largest shells are about nine inches long and they apparently take in quantities of water at one end of the shell and can not only filter out their nutritional requirement but can eject the surplus, at the opposite end, with such force that they become mobile purely by jet propulsion. On the few occasions when the tide recedes so low as to leave them stranded they use the sucking and squirting technique to force their way into the sand away from the hungry seagulls. We had now reached a well populated section of the sea bed, for, at each step we took tiny spurts of water shot up ahead, but after many unsuccessful efforts with the spade I came to the conclusion that if the fish had already squirted it was an absolute waste of time to try to catch up with him, also that if you start to dig down where you see a neat circular hole, about an inch across exactly the same thing applies. However, if you peer intently into the wet sand ahead and see a small portion of shell protruding, he can be yours, providing of course that the slight vibrations, signalled from three oncoming pairs of wellingtons do not make him plunge for safety.

After a series of energetic leaps and dramatic lunges with the spade, our plastic bucket was nearly full so we headed back towards home.

Part of our evening meal the following day was formed by frying diced portions of bacon with razor meat and was deemed to be quite acceptable, interesting and definitely something different, very definitely different.

CHAPTER 14

LARRY THE LAMB

EVERYONE knows the romantic nursery image of playful little lambs, prancing round on the wallpaper, "with fleece as white as snow" we learn. Indeed they are an absolute delight to look at when they are very young, but, one year later, when driven down the hillside they can be looking as grey and almost as bedraggled as the old ewes who had borne them.

Their wet, shaggy, matted wool can get all 'clagged' around their back-ends into hard globules of dung which clatter like a multitude of golf balls as a herd goes jogging by. These poor timid, defenceless creatures would become a heaving mass of maggots unless correctly clipped and totally immersed in disinfectant once a year. This clipping ànd dipping procedure is compulsory throughout the British Isles, but even after that operation has been carried out, the sheep farmer has still such hazards as uncontrolled dogs, foot rot, liver fluke and pulpy kidney to contend with.

At Ballaneddin we had hand reared the exception, Larry, our little orphan was by now a very fine specimen, and looked so fluffy and clean, as if he had been prepared for an agricultural exhibition.

He was just a big cuddly, Toy-town lamb who had certainly thrived upon his upbringing on our Toy-sized farm. He wandered around all day but each night slept on a clean bed of straw. Sometimes, when I sloshed around the outbuildings in the pouring rain to collect the eggs and milk the goat, he would stand within the shelter of the open stable door and watch me, with no intention whatsoever of getting wet himself.

Although there was always an abundance of greenery and hay available he never seemed to miss the slightest opportunity to steal the poultry meal, and at the rear of the house, where the upper half of the stable-type door leading to the kitchen was frequently left open, he would stand on his hind legs and look over the top until given a biscuit or a piece of bread.

He had not grown up in contact with any of his own species but just as a woolly playmate for Tony and maybe regarded himself as much a member of our family as did the sleepy old bulldog bitch. Fay and I enjoyed watching the simple innocence of this contented trio, but, eventually came the day when we had to face the sad reality that this relationship would have to end.

Reluctantly I picked up the telephone directory, looking for an alphabetical entry on the very first page, of the ominous word "ABATTOIR"!

An arrangement was made for the acceptance of one single lamb the following morning and instruction given that a luggage label bearing my name and address be tied round its neck for distinction from the general fatstock entries of the day.

We were thankful that, having reached our decision there was to be no undue delay, no question of sadly counting down poor Larry's remaining days of playtime.

The following morning I folded down the rear seat of the car, lifted in my passenger, and closed the door. Driving towards the Island's capital, Douglas, on that glorious spring morning I felt there was some strange sort of humour in the picture I made while motoring along the roadways with a big woolly lamb standing up behind me surveying the countryside, especially with a luggage label round its neck.

It was only when we were getting near our destination, and Larry moved forward resting his chin on my shoulder, and I felt his warm breath on my cheek, that I became absolutely wretched about the gruesome conclusion that was to end our pleasant relationship.

I turned off the main road and saw a large building ahead which bore a symbolic outline of a bull high up on its brickwork. Close to the structure the route divided, to the left I could see a loading bay and the clinically clean, tiled interior where the white overalled personnel busied themselves handing over the requirements of the waiting butchers.

To the right, I reached the "intake" area and joined the rear of a queue of tall cattle waggons. Switching off the engine, I then heard the pathetic bleating of the lambs and the nervous baying of the tender young beef enclosed within the vehicles that were parked in front, dripping with urine.

The drivers chatted and joked amongst themselves as they waited to disgorge their living cargoes but Larry and I sat quietly alone, waiting our turn.

Stringent legislation is in force these days concerning the welfare of livestock in transit but, of course, all the animals I could see and hear today had only been collected from the Island's farms earlier that same morning. How could any human being estimate the distress that might be within a creature's mind as it looked out through the slatted sides of a transport lorry to see an articulated trailer parked alongside, piled high with the slimy, foul-smelling skins of its already slaughtered fellow creatures? The fresh, familiar aroma of the pure Manx countryside where they had grown up was gone completely now, only the stench of diesel fumes and death remained.

The vehicle immediately ahead eased forward and then reversed towards a concrete ramp, the driver released the tail-board which swung down like a drawbridge. Inside his van were two tall hurdles which each hinged outward to the left and right forming sides, freeing the animals from their confinement and allowing them to timidly feel their footholds down the wooden slats, across to the concrete and straight into the building.

Next came my turn, this was lamb-to-the-slaughter in stark reality, Larry had reached his point of no return, I led him inside the building, signed my name on a form then drove away determined that never again would I become so emotionally involved with any animal that was destined to end up on my dining table.

Two days were allowed for the meat to hang in the cold store and become firm in readiness for cutting before I went along to Douglas again, this time with a clean white sheet in the back of the car, on which to lay the carcase.

Any farmer collecting meat for his own use is requested to do so at a time of the day when he will not hinder the activities of the butchers who queue up to rush their bulk purchases into their shops, for many thousands of lambs each year are processed through the Island's only abattoir. My arrival was rightly timed so I was able to go straight to the loading bay without any delay.

There were rows of pigs, all cleaned and shaven, hanging head downwards from an overhead railway system, there were huge sides of beef and of course the lambs. "One private lamb, Teare, Ballaneddin, please", I called out to a young man looking in my direction. He turned around and made his way along the carcases, examining labels, then reappeared with a stiffened body balanced across his shoulder.

"Do you want the head leaving on?" he asked.

"No thank you", I quickly replied, glancing at the congealed blood swinging in suspension from the nostrils and thinking what on earth would my wife say if I walked into the house with it.

A couple of deft movements with his razor sharp knife soon rectified the matter, then came another question.

"Do you want to take the pluck?" he said, using a term that I did not understand, but was quickly to learn that it applied to a handful of the animals innards, that were kept separately, comprising windpipe, liver, heart, and lungs hanging loosely together as a single unit.

Several of the personnel moved about happily whistling and singing at their work, in fact from deeper within the building I heard a quite acceptable operatic rendering.

Each individual had his or her name, or nickname marked on their white overalls and there seemed to be an atmosphere of efficiency, although everyone seemed so relaxed, pleasant and obliging, not at all like the vegetarian's nightmare of bloodthirsty slaughter house zombies. But, even so, I felt quite relieved to drive away from the place.

CHAPTER 15

ON THE QUAYSIDE

THE holiday-maker or the tax-exile in the Isle of Man can enjoy all the amenities of a glorious off-shore playground but Fay and I did not fall within the golfing, fishing, boating category. We had now created a very comfortable home but one of the nitty-gritty facts of life is the utter impossibility of living blissfully in a happy fairy land without any cash supply coming into the household.

The colourful publicity brochures proclaimed the unspoilt natural beautry, rolling heather clad hills, quiet tree-lined glens, rocky cliffs, sandy beaches, the parks, the castles and other places of historic interest, so readily accessible and more or less freely available. All these details were so very true and so inviting and we certainly looked forward to, in due course, savouring all the enjoyment the Island had to offer.

A Government publication, giving guidance to living on the Isle of Man, had been produced to encourage new residents. It explained the refreshingly low rates of income tax and the complete absence of death duties, discussed matters of investment, pension arrangements and so on, but had been introduced for the encouragement of people contemplating a peaceful and enjoyable retirement, rather than seeking a livelihood. Tax incentives don't exactly lighten the heart of someone who has not yet fathomed out some profit-making form of occupation to even merit the liability for payment of any of this low taxation anyway.

Had I wished to establish some form of industrial activity that would offer employment to local personnel, the Manx Government could have been most generous. Finance could be made available for purchasing, shipping and the installation of machinery, very co-operative terms arranged for factory premises, assistance while training employees, housing of key workers, and so on, even if the overall project would only provide work for a handful of people.

Several interesting prospects came to mind, whether or not any would have been accepted as viable propositions by the Government Office I will not know, for, I was in a frame of mind that bore the very simple requirement of only a modest income, preferably part-time whereby a semi-self-sufficient lifestyle at Ballaneddin could be fully enjoyed. Health and happiness were now our top priorities and peace of mind was not to be disturbed by any furious digging-for-gold activities that seemed to be the prime motivation in life for so many people over in England.

Outside the Island's capital, there are several very picturesque little fishing towns, into which pour the holiday-making sightseers, many arriving by the popular coach excursions that set forth every day from outside the hotels on Douglas promenade.

The ports in the south of the Island are also served by a delightful old steam railway system, the rolling stock of which might seem to have emerged directly from the pages of *Punch*.

Ramsey is the largest of these smaller resorts and lies in the north, where it may be reached by the old-fashioned electric railway line that runs from Douglas, through fields along the cliff-tops for a rickerty-rackerty twenty mile journey of delightful coastal scenery — as one of the most unique forms of public transport still operating anywhere in the British Isles.

Some form of interesting activity could always be seen in Ramsey harbour for it was used not only by the fishing boats but also by the larger vessels bringing in such vital supplies as coal, agricultural equipment and building supplies, without which Island life could be very quickly brought to a standstill. A variety of private pleasure craft eased about silently on their mooring ropes, each giving somebody that pride of ownership whether it be of a luxurious ocean going vessel or just a fibreglass dinghy with an outboard motor suitable for taking one man and a fishing rod for a couple of miles along the coast. (Providing the coastguards had given a suitable weather forecast.)

The buildings around the quayside consisted mostly of warehouses and depots containing agricultural machinery, corn, lime, fertilizer, coal, timber and cement. Although this was the commercial waterfront for the whole of the north of the Island its size hardly detracted from the fishing village charm the tourists loved to see.

Thirsty weatherbeaten seafarers made their way from pub to

pub just as their predecessors had done in the days when they relied on tall masts, canvas sails, and the mercy of the sea, which was so often not forthcoming. The invention of the steam engine meant that when fitted with a propeller a boat then stood a chance of fighting against the wind and getting clear of the rocky coastline. The present-day life of a fisherman with diesel power and intricate electronic aids under his control must be regarded as being so much safer, but, even so it is still a very rough and dangerous life indeed.

In quite a central position along the Western Quayside I noticed a small single storey warehouse had become disused, this aroused my interest and I learnt that the key was available from an estate agent's office, where I was told, "It has been in use as a paint store and workshop for the past twenty years but prior to that had been a coal depot with a stable at the rear".

Situated in the centre of the frontage was a large door that could be rolled open on cast iron wheels to allow the horse drawn coal carts of years gone by to pass in and out. The key that Fay and I had collected opened a small door at the side and we stepped into what had once been an office with a window looking out onto a rectangular mark on the concreted roadway where there had once been a weighing platform. Inside the office there had been a system of levers whereby the operator could read out the weight of the cart or lorry standing outside. The rest of the interior of the empty building was dull, damp and depressing, panes of glass were broken in the windows and in one corner a tap dripped water onto the floor, where the original old cobblestones had been partially concreted over.

Had we not already experienced the months of grit and rubble that had preceded the creation of our country dream-home, I'm sure we would have retreated in dismay, handing back the key without any further consideration. The building certainly looked very grim but we had reached the position where even the most remote proposition must at least be given consideration. One cannot live on goats milk and bantam's eggs indefinitely.

Ramsey already had a street of busy little shops running parallel to the quayside, back to back with the old coal yard. If that same floor area had been available on the main thoroughfare it would have been of considerable value.

Could shoppers be encouraged to walk around the corner?

When the holiday coaches unloaded, the womenfolk would always surge towards the toilets and then the shops, but the more persistent of the reluctant husbands would manage to break away to walk patiently up and down looking at the boats, and maybe take a quick sip of the local brew.

If we could possibly create some form of retail premises on the quayside to hold the interest of all the family, our own personal problem would be solved. Suppose we served refreshments too? Suppose the whole building was given a mammoth spring clean and the walls all whitewashed? Could it become a quayside market?

Quite a challenge!

CHAPTER 16

INTO BUSINESS

THE application for the change of use and structural alterations to the quayside property duly received the blessing of the Ramsey Planning Committee and eventually the conveyancing documents were drawn up and completed by the appropriate signing and witnessing procedure.

Although there was a Market Square, it was now used solely as a car park and the pictures I had seen, of boatloads of fish being sold off on the cobble-stones, seemed to date back at least half a century.

I made appropriate enquiries and established that there was no reason why the newly acquired premises could not be proclaimed as being a "market". I felt that the word itself would arouse a certain amount of interest amongst potential money spenders, though at this stage it had not been decided what precise commodities should be offered to the public.

The shipping onto the Island of such things as pots and pans, clothing, crockery and so on should not present much difficulty beyond the obvious expenditure involved by the actual transportation. Living on a small island does mean that so very many commodities are likely to cost fractionally more, in fact Fay had already found certain of her recent purchases to be considerably higher in price than the identical articles available in England, sometimes to such an extent that it could not possibly be accounted for by carriage charges. Perhaps those particular items of merchandise could produce the business opening we were looking for?

The roof timbers were hefty and quite sound, looking upwards on the inside was not unlike a chapel but, unfortunately they all carried a long standing accumulation of coal dust. Standing at the top of a ladder I began to laboriously brush the stuff away and the whole building was quickly full of floating dust that got in my eyes, my ears, my hair, up my nostrils and caked around the moisture of my lips. Several times I came home looking like a rather tired sore-eyed minstrel, but at least I was making progress and the sooner I got the premises ready for trading, the better.

The dry brushing process was then followed up with a brushing and hose-piping action along the beams and down the walls, so when I came down the ladder for the final time the floor was awash with filthy black sludge and the one and only drain inside the building was blocked up.

Arrangements were made for the plumbing and the electrical work to be carried out, buckets and buckets full of whitewash were slapped against the walls, each with its little old fashioned

bag of dolly-blue added in a hope for that whiter than white look and in a few days the whole place was dried out and looking quite different.

Every day that this work had been going on the large sliding door onto the quayside had been wide open so the activities had aroused a great deal of curiosity, speculation and the inevitable Manx humour, but out of all this however, I was able to sift through the opinions of a cross section of the community who normally spent much of their time around the town.

Fay and I reached the conclusion that there seemed to be a very definite need not only in Ramsey, but also throughout the Island, for the cheaper end of the clothing trade, such as anoraks, jeans, T-shirts, just the sort of lines that you'd expect to find on market stalls across the water. Supplies could be very easily arranged for I had sufficient connections in fashion and textiles to obtain anything between babies' nappies and mink coats. Our premises were by no means sophisticated, still just an old warehouse on the dockside that had been tidied up a bit and the only way to test its potential was by trial and error, with actual stock.

I had finished the joinery needed to incorporate a small snackbar within the building and by simply sawing a door in half horizontally so the top half could be swung open independently, ice-cream and sandwiches could be sold directly to the holidaymakers standing outside on the quay in summertime. My brother and his young sons had come over to visit us, to whom I was pleased to supply paint brushes, and the finishing touches were speeded up considerably.

An arrangement was made for a small selection of ladies garments to be put on an aircraft at Manchester and a short while later we collected them from the Island airport and headed back to Ramsey. Carrying the cardboard boxes into the building aroused the interest of passers-by and a couple of people actually walked into the building and watched us opening them up. The first to be opened contained a couple of dozen skirts of assorted colours and materials. I picked the invoice out of the box and as Fay read out the style numbers off tickets attached to each garment I added a reasonable profit and quoted her a selling price, whereupon one of the by-standers asked the size of a certain skirt and then, to our absolute amazement handed over the money to make a purchase.

Hurray! We were in business straight away. Fay was actually a qualified beautician and hair-dresser, who had never worked in a shop in her life, so she was absolutely thrilled, especially as she sold a further three garments in the course of the same afternoon.

So far, so good. It certainly appeared from our initial experience that, provided the correct type of stock was on the premises, the "Quayside Market" could be regarded as a viable proposition. If all went well we might possibly gain the comparatively small income we needed by trading in Ramsey just on Fridays and Saturdays, and enjoying our rusticated lifestyle for the rest of the week.

Purchasing a reasonable selection of stock would require the co-operation of the local bank, so I made an appointment to go and see the manager. He was a jovial giant of a man, who, having seen my account diminish considerably in the course of the structural projects in town and country, did not seem at all surprised that I should now be in need of his assistance.

When he was a youngster he had lived near Ballaneddin; he remembered collecting milk each day, had seen the farm in its fullest efficiency, then in the tragic state of neglect and had now, already expressed his pleasure at seeing the more recent change of fortune. As I placed my signature on the piece of paper, staking my home as colateral in order to set up the business, he quietly said, "I hope I never see the day", and I know he spoke truly from his heart.

No sooner had we begun to congratulate ourselves on the straightforward way that our affairs had slotted nicely into position and had become resigned to the fact that we were about to start a venture from scratch, carrying with us such necessary evils as two private mortgages and a bank loan, than we received an important looking envelope from the Government Offices, Douglas.

The curt instruction it contained, to cease trading immediately, was a bit bothering under the circumstances, but happily it was only a temporary set-back, I had simply been unaware that the plan submitted to the Town Hall at Ramsey, should also have been presented for the consideration of Government Planning Office, Douglas.

Soon we were enjoying the best of two entirely different activities, for most of the week we were at peace in the countryside with our livestock around us, then for a couple of days we were members of the business community and pleased to join in the cheerful back-chat of a happy trader-customer relationship. I think that because it was known as a "market" rather than an actual shop, some people felt quite at liberty to walk in through the open door, just for a chat and a legpull, with no particular intention of buying anything.

CHAPTER 17

LES LAPINS

THOUSANDS upon thousands of wild rabbits must exist on the Island, judging by the numbers of casualties seen on the roadways every day, and they are an absolute pest on some farms. On a clear dry night, with a powerful handlamp and a good working dog, up to a hundred rabbits can be bagged. This "lamping" is discouraged by law because of the disturbance caused to sheep, in any case unless one has a satisfactory arrangement for the speedy shipment to a butcher in England there is very little demand upon the Island. Many of the population recall rabbit stew and rabbit pie as wartime economy meals or merely as a relief from the basic spuds and herring dishes still remembered from the times when there wasn't today's prosperity to enjoy.

Although there were many of these furry little bunnies living amongst the brambles and gorse up our own hillside it was much easier for me to accept the invitation from a friend who farmed along the coast further north to go whenever I wished to shoot them in his fields.

The cooking procedure for wild rabbit must always start by putting the pieces into cold water, bringing them to the boil then pouring away the liquid, this is called "blanching" and is done purely to reduce that strong rabbity flavour but, even so, the finished dishes never seemed to compare with the succulent meals I had enjoyed in so many households on the continent. The difference is, of course, that over there they are using domestically reared animals, young and tender, specially bred for table use, and not to be even confused with the children's pets who seem to sit contentedly in hutches for several years on a diet of dandelion and lettuce leaves pushed to them by sticky little fingers.

So the next addition to our Toy-town farming life was to be some top quality basic breeding stock for the production of our own Ballaneddin rabbit meat. The characteristics required were to be, rapid growth, freedom from and resistance to disease, plus a good food conversion ratio, this meaning that plenty of meat would be produced in relation to the foodstuff consumed, the object being to produce healthy meaty youngsters with a light bone structure that would reach a weight of about four pounds within the tender age of eight weeks. Although Fay would be having nothing whatsoever to do with the sad necessity of knocking these baby animals on the back of the neck, she certainly looked forward to a regular supply of bonny little carcasses of white meat, rather than be expected to produce gastronomic delicacies from the older, tougher, scraggy little country cousins that I had brought in full of lead shot, tufts of fur, congealed blood and splintered bones. I told her the difference would be like comparing spring chicken with an old crow. Not that we had ever had old crow on our menu, but I once plucked and dressed one very neatly and presented it to a friend of ours as *corbeau de l'isle fantastique*, and not surprisingly she failed to find it mentioned in any cook book.

Commercial rabbit breeding had already become established in England so to buy my initial stock I could take advantage of all the years of painstaking research and the cross-breeding of heavy varieties from America, New Zealand and elsewhere, and the detailed recording of sires and dams over very many animal generations, whereby hybrid specimens had been produced that

would rear consistently good litters of youngsters that were virtually fat-free, had a rapid growth rate, a high resistance to disease and an exceptional good meat to bone ratio.

Ordering one young buck and one unrelated young doe that was already in kindle to a sire outside either family meant that from the first litter to be born I could retain females to join their mother in a productive harem that would not only produce all our own table requirements, but would give me an insight into the potential for a rabbit farm on the Island. I certainly had buildings that could be quite easily adapted for that purpose but whether or not there would be sufficient households who were aware of the superior culinary potential of my tender hand reared carcasses than the obvious limitations of the multitude of wild creatures so easily available from the hillsides, I had yet to find out.

Using a roll of the type of galvanised netting that is formed of one inch squares, cutting it into sections and then clipping them together with a specially shaped pair of pliers, it was quite easy to assemble a line of fattening cages and breeding pens, all raised clear from the cold stone floor of the barn. To each one I attached a food hopper for containing a carefully balanced diet of dried meal and a drinking system whereby each animal had access to water from inverted wine bottles.

At a pre-arranged time we set off by car to the airport as a family threesome, each eager to see our new purchases. Driving around to the air-freight section, where I had previously collected large cartons of goods for sale on our Quayside Market I found that the airport personnel were already making speculative remarks about the two cardboard boxes marked "LIVESTOCK, HANDLE WITH CARE" which had been carried in off the tarmac amongst the cargo a few minutes earlier.

We opened up the lids and saw two beautiful, snow white bunnies in excellent condition, each with its registration number on ear tags that were pink for the girl and blue for the boy. I signed a form to indicate that the consignment had been received in undamaged state and soon the little animals were on their way to their future home.

They had both been immunised against myxomatosis so, although their life was to be restricted within four sides of a cage, one could be consoled with the fact that they had not only never known green fields, they would never end up sitting at a roadside with swollen head and bulging eyes awaiting death like the wild members of the species, whenever the dreaded disease swept through different areas of the Island.

The estimated production per doe on a well managed establishment was said to be fifty youngsters per year so another aspect of our Ballaneddin way of life was already under way. Apart from the meat value there was also the potential use of pelts for the manufacture of clothes, cuddly toys and other novelties, and of course a useful supply of garden fertilizer, but I was not going to get carried away with the furtherance of this, as portrayed in some American publications whereby dried and ground rabbit currents become a money spinning powder when sold in plastic bags at garden shops. Another so-called side-line of commercial rabbit keeping is said to be the breeding of earthworms amongst the droppings below the cages, for retail as fishing bait, but I could not imagine any of my Manx fishing acquaintances handing over money when they can so easily dig their own lugworm off the beach.

Had our rabbits read all the recommendations that are laid out for any person going into commercial activity they might have

been rather disillusioned with the Isle of Man, for much importance is given to a controlled temperature, within a fly-proof and draught-proof building, into which the entry of cats, kids and dogs is strictly prohibited. On the contrary their new accommodation was very much aligned with the general comings and goings of everyday farmyard life. The balanced diet, carefully weighed out and supplied in pellet form seemed very good in theory and was so clean and simple for the white coated attendants in the clinical conditions of the specialised breeding depots, but from now on, although maintaining a balance, they would also be introduced to nourishment in its more basic form such as turnips, cabbages and hay, according to economic availability.

How ironical it is that the humble little animal's habits should be darkened with the expression "breed like rabbits" so commonly associated with the birth explosion in our over populated world, with an ever increasing problem of grave food shortage. No matter how enthusiastic the creatures may seem, the female does not bear young unless conditions are suitable and if circumstances should change, there is within her body the remarkable ability to terminate a pregnancy by the re-absorbtion of the embryos.

IF PEOPLE BRED LIKE RABBITS,
THEY WOULDN'T STARVE LIKE HUMANS!

CHAPTER 18

A NEW MARSHAL

THE Island's holiday season starts at the beginning of May when boat fares and accommodation charges are reduced to encourage groups of pensioners and over-sixties clubs, plus anyone else who wishes to make an early visit before the schools break up for summer, when the weather can be reasonably warm but the Island is still quiet and peaceful. Coaches would bring these people into Ramsey for day trips and they would wander slowly round the shops, usually in couples who had many years of work behind them, others walking quietly alone,.with well worn wedding rings, cherishing memories of a departed partner but so glad to have grown-up children and grandchildren to whom they can send post cards. They would troop along the quayside, see our signwriting on the wall and then walk through the door with words that I've heard time and time again of "OOQH, what a little market!" in accents that indicated that they had expected premises the size they knew at home in Manchester, Birmingham or some other big city, and then proceed to pick up our neatly displayed garments, examine them closely, hold them against each other and then put them down again.

This might go on for half an hour, especially if it was raining outside, at the end of which time the whole place would look like a jumble sale, but this was all part of their holiday, they didn't usually buy anything, generally because they just hadn't got the money to spare. In the years that were to come we knew very well that the only requirements of those early season coach-loads of old folks would be very simply a cup of tea, the use of a toilet, two or three picture post cards of Ramsey and maybe the odd cheap souvenir ashtray bearing the three-legged emblem or the Manx tail-less cat.

The last week of the month however, starts the build-up to the greatest sporting spectacle in the world when the most skilful and most daring of young racing men come onto the Isle of Man to start practising for the International Tourist Trophy Motor Cycle Races, willingly risking their lives to achieve a very coveted winner's title in the "MANX T.T.", the most prestigious event in the motorcycling calendar.

A week of practising is so very essential, for these are "road races" and as such are vastly different to any racing done on disused airports or purpose built short circuits. The course starts from the outskirts of Douglas, going due west across the Island, then north past the entrance to Ballaneddin and on to Ramsey. In front of the Town Hall the riders turn right sharply then go speeding out of town, up the mountain road to a height of over a thousand feet above sea level and steeply down the other side back into Douglas again. Each lap is thirty-seven miles along country roads, through picturesque villages, but every dwelling, every garden wall and every tree along the route is a hazard to be avoided. Hundreds of bales of straw are placed in position at the most treacherous corners and placards are erected to indicate the nature of the turn but most important of all is the racing man's experience and knowledge of the entire course and to anticipate even every gear change. The words "tourist trophy" can be rather misleading for someone who has no knowledge of the Island or of its famous motorcycling event, I'm sure many people don't realise that these lads go round this tortuous country circuit for lap after lap at average speeds that exceed a hundred miles an hour.

To the normal four wheel family motorist this must sound an absolute suicidal impossibility but every year there are far more applications for entry into the races than can possibly be accepted. No-one is allowed to compete in the T.T. unless he has already proved his racing ability elsewhere and even so, must achieve a stipulated qualifying time during the practice week otherwise his race entry is cancelled. This is called a tourist race but there is no question whatsoever of a rider sitting up-right and reading the road as it comes towards him. He must remember every twist in those thirty-seven miles; his life depends on it.

Most of the warning signs and bales of straw are left in position during the summer, for the course comes into use again at the end of August when there is another practice week followed by a race-week, the Manx Grand Prix. The professional riders using the very latest works developments in racing machinery are excluded from these events, giving the up and coming youngster the chance to earn international acclaim. Many of whom have invested every penny they could get hold of to gain a machine worthy of the Manx circuit and arrive here virtually on a shoestring, but anyone watching a Grand Prix winner can be seeing some future world champion taking a very positive step towards joining the big rich league of international racing stars.

Obviously the roads are closed to all other traffic for several hours each day of these racing periods; cattle, sheep and horses are securely impounded and every householder living near the circuit has to tolerate the inconvenience of being a prisoner within their own premises, having temporary disruption of postal deliveries, milk supplies and so on, plus the anxiety imposed upon all cat or dog owners bearing responsibility to keep their pet secured at all times, for fear of the most horrific consequences.

The members of the Manx police force and all their part-time special constables are on duty for long tiring hours during these times and I'm sure their tolerance is stretched to the absolute limit. The whole operation would not be possible however, without a very stalwart band of volunteers who act as race marshalls, for every time the riders go out on the course there are dozens of people sheltering in hedges, leaning over stone walls, sacrificing their time, often in wind and rain, to ensure that the roadways are clear and to give assistance in the event of any accident. For over half a century motor bikes have been racing on the Isle of Man and marshalls have always been on duty, to many people the annual offering of their services has become almost a ritual, some even take their annual holiday time from work to coincide with the events, as their personal contribution to a world famous sporting occasion, for which they receive no remuneration whatsoever beyond their own personal satisfaction.

I went into Ramsey Police Station and offered my services for, I'd learned in the local press and from Manx Radio that this was the day for all potential marshalls to gather at convenient parts of the Island for the official "swearing in" sessions, when each person accepted for duty is vested with certain powers and responsibilities something like being a Special Constable, but applicable only to a precise period of time and on a pre-determined length of the circuit.

Arriving back home I pulled an official marshall's armband out of my pocket and, sliding it into position up my sleeve, marched through the doorway, but assured my wife that I would not allow the status of my official appointment to affect our relationship in any way. She could still address me by my Christian name in private.

There was no frivolity whatsoever a few days later when I set out to take up my very first duty, it was four-thirty in the morning, I'd had a cup of tea, stuck an apple in my pocket and was now driving towards my pre-arranged section by one of the T.T.'s landmarks, the Sulby Glen Hotel, part way along the very fast "Sulby Straight". Ballaneddin was only about a mile along the road that snaked its way through the tree-lined zig-zags of "Quarry bends", but the roads were to be closed to traffic by four-forty and prior to that time I was to see that no obstructions had come onto the racing line during the night in the form of twigs, dead rabbits or hedgehogs, or even sheets of paper that could endanger the fellows who would be at that time warming up their machines in the pit area outside Douglas, nearly twenty miles away.

The hotel was at a crossroads, facing the village post-office on one corner and a Methodist chapel on the other. I parked the car around the back and then closed the two side roads by stretching across the lengths of rope that had been lying nearby for that purpose, each with a small piece of red rag dangling from the centre to be quickly seen in the very unlikely event of any motorist coming along at that time of day.

There wasn't another person in sight, although marshalls operate in pairs whenever possible, the morning sunshine was glorious, the air was still cool but so fresh and clean, apart from the sound of the birds there was absolute silence and stillness. Standing quietly there, wearing my armband I felt rather alone, at what was normally the focal point of the little community, and began to wonder what might happen during my tour of duty and to turn over memories of First Aid classes attended many years ago, not feeling very confident and hoping earnestly that nothing would go wrong that morning. Everything was so absolutely quiet I even wondered whether I might be standing at the right place at the right time, but on the wrong date.

Then a figure stepped into the road a couple of hundred yards away and raised an arm, I waved in reply, quite relieved that I had a colleague on duty. Shortly afterwards a police van went by, pausing to see that both barrier ropes were in position and acknowledging my own existence with a friendly nod.

A few minutes later came the unmistakable sound of a distant motor-bike then into view came the rider, he was certainly going at a fast cruising speed but sitting bolt upright. On his back was a big letter "M', he was a "travelling marshall". By riding from point to point and reporting by telephone the team of travelling marshalls could, within a few minutes survey the complete course and assure the officials at the start by phone that it was alright to let the first of the competitors get away in pairs at ten second intervals.

I walked up and down a little distance to keep my feet warm and had started biting at my apple when another sound came through the morning air. This time it was a highly tuned, multi-cylindered piece of racing machinery screaming up and down through the gears, then bursting out of Quarry Bends like a howling banshee.

The rider was tucked in tightly behind his streamlining with his chest down onto the fuel tank as he flashed between myself and the Post Office at no less than an incredible one hundred and forty miles an hour and, guess what? HE WAS ONLY PRACTISING!

CHAPTER 19

MAD SUNDAY

THE final practice session was over and the riders were taking a slight respite, but their individual lap times had been reported over the radio and through the press to the thousands of fans who were now converging upon the Island on the boats that ran a day and night shuttle service from Liverpool and Heysham. Many had travelled across Europe, some had come halfway round the world, they were the motor cycle purists to whom racing men and machines formed a very important part of their life. The ship's decks were covered with these leatherclad pilgrims sailing to the motor-cycle Mecca, filling the air with "bike talk" all the way over.

The first race of the programme had started on Saturday but by Sunday morning, over ten thousand motorcycles had been landed on the Douglas quayside. This mass assembly of two wheeled enthusiasts must in no way whatsoever be associated with the affairs concerning the so-called Mods and Rockers that take place in England, indeed such people are almost non-existent. Maybe they are not quite sure whether hooliganism is still punishable by a few strokes of the birch in the Isle of Man.

Many of the visitors have attended the races time and time again, indeed some head straight for the Police Headquarters in Douglas to offer their services as marshalls, others, across for the first time are fulfilling a lifetime ambition, but whether it be first visit or twenty-first every single one of them will want to ride round and round the circuit on Sunday, well known to the residents of the Island as MAD SUNDAY.

The roads are not closed to normal traffic, all the usual restrictions and regulations are applicable, but to be astride a machine on an actual race course gives such a tremendous temptation to open up the throttle. Although the Island's police force is spread around to slow these fellows down at various danger points, most of the course is through open country without a speed limit and once they've been round a couple of times many of them find it very difficult to supress an urge to actually race each other, between the bobbies. Most residents keep well away from these thirty-seven miles of roadway on Mad Sunday, or else they stand at some safe viewpoint just to observe the great volume of traffic, for, not only are the motorcyclists circulating in mass, there are also hundreds of private cars and just about every luxury coach available on the Island. Sometimes the flow will be restricted while a coach full of fans cruises its way cautiously through a series of bends, and in that short space of time up to a hundred 'bikes can have caught it up and are revving eagerly behind, waiting for the next length of straight roadway to overtake and go snarling down the road like packs of wolves. This is very dangerous and I certainly wouldn't dream of driving a car in the opposite direction, although of course I'd be fully entitled to, except for part of the mountain road which has been made one-way-only during recent years.

The fans come from all round the world because the Manx T.T. racing is so unique, and I'm sure that tens of thousands of spectators are not allowed to surge round and round the Silverstone, Indianapolis or Nurnburg circuits at high speed between the race days. Accidents do happen of course, but it must be very difficult for the owner of a fast machine to realise how dangerous it can be to travel at eighty miles an hour down a fast stretch of the mountain, knowing full well that the particular racing man he idolises will reach double that figure later in the week.

Apart from the grandstand at the start and finish line and a little terraced seating on some corners near Douglas, the rest of the course constitutes absolutely free entertainment, so, on Sunday as this huge circus goes milling round the Island people are continually turning off, stopping and trying to select which is to be the favourite spot to watch the following day's racing, whether it be lying on a grass bank, sitting on a stone wall or leaning over a field gate, with the machines passing only an arm's length away.

Many would pull up at Ramsey and stretch their legs around the harbour for a little while and we found it well worth offering refreshment for sale at the Market kiosk. Each year we drove cautiously out of the Ballaneddin driveway onto the main road, while the majority of visitors were still having breakfast in Douglas or perhaps finishing cornflakes outside the little tents that had popped up overnight, and we hurried along to Ramsey in a trickle of traffic that would become an absolute torrent as the day went on.

The pair of us were kept quite busy supplying hot dogs, hamburgers, sandwiches, ice-cream and soft drinks to a very happy-go-lucky but well behaved multinational clientele. Occasionally someone would wish to buy an extra sweater or perhaps replace a damaged pair of denim jeans, but generally speaking the T.T. enthusiasts had little room to take home any additional luggage.

Within the motor-cycling fraternity is a small but very dedicated group called the "sidecar people", almost a breed of their own, whose racing outfits are three-wheeled mechanical monstrosities, drawing board rejects, projects most unlikely to succeed, but they introduce a rugged he-man element into a week of otherwise neat and stylish high speed riding.

They have small wheels to bring the machinery as low to the ground as possible but big wide tyres that are to take atrocious punishment on the road, for, once the two man crew have pushed their vehicle away from the starting line and the engine fires, the driver dives into his kneeling position and from then onwards he must wrestle for every inch of the way to keep his bouncing, lurching, ungainly racer within the walls and hedges at a hundred miles an hour. He's riding on the back of a grotesque three legged wounded crab that goes utterly beserk at the twist of a throttle.

The passenger facilities are simply an aluminium platform with some metal hand holds and the driver is well aware that, as they hurtle towards a bend together, unless his courageous colleague throws his full weight onto the correct side as a counterbalance, the pair of them will smash straight into the nearest obstruction.

Likewise, as the passenger hangs his body right away from the vehicle to gain maximum leverage he must have full confidence in his partner's judgement and ability to steer within inches of bone splintering hazards. These competitors have to be extrmely fit and alert, I understand that even a quite good stretch of roadway like the Sulby Straight resembles cobblestone when taken at full speed. At the end of a few gruelling laps both driver and passenger are completely exhausted with the shaking and bruising they've taken. Awareness of this physical exertion, coupled with the overall danger involved makes it quite incredible to read the race programme and occasionally see a lady named as passenger, sometimes even a husband and wife teaming together in a dance of death. My own nephew raced successfully as a passenger on English circuits but I was very relieved when he retired before I had the sickening anxiety of watching him set off to career round the Isle of Man on what had at one time been his ambition.

The traffic would ease off a little around teatime, so we would leave the Ramsey quayside and head for home. Not driving against the stream but taking side lanes that lead us to a point beyond our farm entrance where we could join the general flow of vehicles and then break off with safety.

Once we returned home to find that a tent had been erected near our entrance, from which came laughter and French conversation. I went across and chatted with a merry foursome who had left their homes on Friday, crossed the Channel overnight, driven up through England on their two motorbikes, sailed from Liverpool, arrived on the Island in the early hours, done a few laps of the course, then pitched their tent. Most of the laughter however was about their own ridiculous predicament, finding the English banks all closed on Saturday and likewise in the Isle of Man on Sunday they'd run completely out of food. Anyhow, they certainly enjoyed Fay's cooking and a couple of bottles of home made wine as our guests that evening.

We accepted any sort of currency at the market, providing a newspaper quoted its rate of exchange but I heard of a quite amusing incident about a group of German motorcyclists who thought they had assembled outside a "bank" they had located in the country waiting for it to open. Eventually the occupant came forth and had to explain to them that the wording on his sign that read "ELLEN BANK NURSERIES" had nothing whatsoever to do with foreign exchange.

CHAPTER 20

RACE WEEK

RECENT happenings had seemed to be so very far removed from the peaceful lifestyle we cherished, but the motorcycle events that were to take place annually past our gateway contribute so greatly to the tourist industry and in turn to the entire economy of the Island, that any inconvenience caused needed to be tolerated with patience by all concerned, for just a few more days.

The practising was over, the fans were here, every hotel and boarding house was packed to capacity but the local radio kept appealing for further accommodation. Machines were parked solidly abreast along the Douglas Promenade, hundreds more were lined up along the side roads, enthusiasts walked up and down for the sheer enjoyment of studying such a vast array of machinery assembled in one great world-wide collection.

The preliminaries were over, in the morning brave young men would step into a thirty-seven mile arena to put their machines and personal ability to the test. They had ample opportunity to examine the entire course and to practice upon it; they had seen the hazards and it was up to each individual to avoid them, not to ride as fast as his machine would travel, but as fast as his own judgement and skill allowed, in circumstances that concerned other riders, varying types of road surface, and changes in weather conditions. Unless there happened to be some mechanical defect, if a rider took the wrong line or travelled too fast in the wrong place and had an accident, it must be regarded as his own lack of judgement. "The twist-grip operates both ways" is a common but rather heartless expression, but, whatever one's sympathies, it is such an absolute fact.

Unfortunately, fatalities do take place but one must accept that up to the split second before the moment of impact the rider concerned had been enjoying the most thrilling, exhilarating race of his life, and his pals might even say that this was the way he would have liked to have left them.

Our original hopes had been to secure the moderate income we required solely by weekend trading but we had already realised the necessity to take advantage of what was the Isle of Man's busiest period of the year and to open our doors to the public every day during race week. Several of the schools are situated actually at the side of the T.T. course or quite close by, so much so that it is necessary for them to be closed. This was to our advantage for we were able to incorporate the services of a couple of schoolgirls as sales assistants. A pair of spindly fair haired sisters, the first of a series of pleasant, willing young helpers who came to us as little girls playing shop with real money but with whom we had a very happy family relationship and in due course were quite proud to see them mature and blossom forth into attractive young ladies pursuing their respective occupations.

The Education Authority is concerned with the welfare of youngsters who wish to work during their school holidays and they had to be assured that my little slaves were not to be employed in a slaughterhouse, public bar or betting office, nor would they be exposed to dangerous machinery or chemicals. In actual fact the main qualifications for anyone working in our little market were simple honesty, common sense and good humour (especially on a wet day when we would all run round with pans and buckets to stop the water dripping through the roof from falling onto our stock).

Sometimes we would hear Manx Radio announce that the start of racing had been delayed because of mist on the mountain and that a further announcement would be made in half an hour. This meant that all the thousands of spectators positioned around the Island would have to wait with their cameras, sandwiches and transistor radios, everyone hoping that the weather would clear. Perhaps the next announcement might be of a further half hour delay and be received with a gigantic unanimous groan from the fans, and I'm sure it must increase the tension within the competitors' compound.

Then, we would hear that the race was definitely on, the national anthem was being played and the first two men were in position on the starting line, the long wait is all forgotten and everyone looks down the road for the riders to come into sight.

Occasionally the weather can cause the cancellation of an entire day's programme, this is unfortunate for the events have to be rescheduled within the few precious days available, and the disappointed fans must solemnly make their way back to boarding houses and camp sites, some of whom will only then become aware of the fact that not only are the public houses on the Island open all day long, but also that the spirits are served from much larger optics.

Apart from the road-racing, all the other aspects of motorcycle sport are planned to take place within the confines of the rocky coastline. There's moto-cross, trial riding, racing on grass and also on sand, plus very dignified Vintage Rallies, where quite a remarkable range of museum pieces go sedately along the road with a "pop-pop-pop" from engines that still transmit their power through leather belts.

Providing everything was running smoothly in the Market I used to enjoy slipping away for half an hour to cross over the harbour via the swing bridge to watch the "sprint" races along the promenade.

Some of the classes are for the visitor who thinks that his own particular machine can do very well when accelerated over an absolutely straight quarter of a mile; other events are for contraptions with huge rear tyres, flimsy looking lightweight front wheels and big engines fitted into mountings drilled full of holes for further weight reduction. They appear out of transit vans which are veritable mobile workshops to not only tune and maintain the sprint racing machines but also designed to bring these high-compression engines to life by an arrangement of rollers propelled by the engine of the van.

Lots of gatherings take place at pre-arranged venues of motorcycle clubs and various organisations where members are united by the common individual ownership of a specific make of machine. The B.S.A. Owners Club usually met at the side of the lake in Ramsey so this was an occasion when, subject to Fay and the girls having everything under control, I would don my helmet and potter along astride my old 250 cc to park it alongside other old-timers, all polished into showroom condition.

So, with all these activities going on, together with the normal entertainment of a seaside resort, the Isle of Man is, for those few days an absolute motorcyclist's paradise, throbbing with excitement.

When the last of the back-markers of each day's racing has gone down the road, along comes the "ROADS OPEN" car. This is always a fast sports car that carries out one complete lap of the course, bearing a notice indicating that the highways now resort to normal conditions. As the driver goes screeching round every blind corner and hurtling across every halt sign with legalised privilege, he must be the envy of the multitude of car owners who wave him on. Then, in Douglas, comes the presentation of awards to the riders of the day, and the fans disperse to talk about the records that have been broken, the successes and the failures, where the casual expression that some individual "Threw it down the road" can actually mean that the person concerned probably came off at near a hundred miles an hour, but thanks to the leathers he wore and maybe a couple of straw bales, he was able to walk away from it. These racing men are like steeplechase jockeys to whom the occasional broken bone is just an occupational hazard.

After the final race of the week, the sports car roars through the town, the barriers are all taken down and within half an hour Ramsey has returned once more to peaceful normality.

The great evacuation is now in progress, every available vessel in Douglas harbour taking on-board cars and motorbikes to absolute capacity. A very large number of people are soon on their way home from a wonderful holiday, during which they have enjoyed a free display of the finest road racing in the world.

Unfortunately, there will be a few who remain behind, in hospital, and some journalists seem to find a ready market for articles on blood-shed in the Isle of Man, invariably totting up the number of fatalities that have taken place in more than half a century. This is a very sad and disturbing statistic, but comparisons with other international events are meaningless unless one takes into full consideration the fact that the Manx Tourist Trophy races involve the covering of over thirty thousand miles in very high speed practice, followed by fifty thousand miles of actual racing. The circuit is very demanding both for man and machine, but each year there are far more applications for entry than can possibly be accepted.

The happy-go-lucky foursome from France who had camped near Ballaneddin called, to thank us for our hospitality before their departure. One couple had proudly shown us photos of the two young children they had left behind with Grandma, the family had never been parted before for so long, and they were now eagerly looking forward to getting back home again.

Two wheeled motor vehicles are precarious machines to handle at any time, whether it be in a form of sport, or simply as an economic form of transport. Fay and I had a saddening awareness of the vulnerability of the people who ride them when we learned that the following day a tragic accident had taken place on a motorway in England . . .

Those young homeward bound parents had both been killed.

CHAPTER 21

PIGLETS

PROGRESS towards our country style of ideal living had been brought to an abrupt standstill during the two weeks that had been so dominated by circulating motorcycles, coupled with our personal necessity to make hay on the quayside while the opportunity was there.

Following the exodus of the racing people there is always a slight lull in tourist activities until the end of the month when the Island's accommodation begins to fill up again for the peak month of July. This respite gave opportunity to incorporate pig-keeping into our small-scale farming unit.

The old stone-pig-sties were reasonably sound but the doors had rotted away long long ago, and the small open air yard that each animal would have access to was filled completely with nettles and brambles. The floor both inside and outside the sties was simply bare soil, no drainage, no possibility of flushing out with a hose pipe, so, although a dry bed of straw and wood-shavings could be offered under cover, the open air pen would become a mixture of mud and pig muck, deepening according to the number of pigs and the amount of rainfall.

The obvious solution would be with the use of concrete but as access could only be gained by climbing over the stone wall and then entering into the buildings by crawling on hands and knees, this would mean clambering back and forth and crawling in and out, a bucketful at a time. A cubic yard of wet concrete weighs nearly two tons so each bucketful is probably close to a hundred-weight, the more I thought about it, the more I realised the amount of back-ache the operation could entail.

I had already seen five fine looking piglets that were for sale, so decided that the old fashioned sties could be used just as a temporary measure until I could put down a layer of concrete in one of the other buildings, where a readymixed lorryload could be delivered straight into the doorway, to be spread and smoothed down in a speedy burst of activity. Even so, with this short-cut flooring one must be careful not to order the delivery of a greater quantity of this wet, messy, heavy substance than one is capable of dispersing within a couple of hours.

Fay and I drove along to negotiate the transaction that was to increase our stock-holding considerably, we knew they were part of a good healthy litter, we knew the asking price and were travelling with five sacks in readiness, but before any deal is made there needs to be long standing ritual whereby the prospective purchaser lapses into complete silence, then slowly takes a deep breath and utters – "How-little-will-you-take?"

Agreement was duly reached and we were soon driving home to quickly unload our wriggling packages before they soiled the vehicle too much. Frequently in some parts of England, when a transaction is made between country-folk it concludes with the handing back of a little "luck money", as sort of unwritten discount, but I don't think this applies in that manner in the Isle of Man, also, in England the bargaining procedure will frequently include mention of the fact that payment is going to be offered in "cash" but this incentive is of little interest in a country with such a reasonable income tax rate (20% maximum).

Weaning takes place between two and three months from birth and is a critical period of the youngster's life, pigs weaned too early soon go down-hill. We were very pleased with our purchases, they settled into their new surroundings quickly and were soon frisking mischievously about in the straw. All pigs are very clean by nature and, whatever sort of accommodation they become restricted within, they will always endeavour to soil only one corner, furtherst away from their bedding. To see clean healthy weaners with silvery bristles glistening over their pink skins playing happily together, makes one wonder what thoughts less fortunate pigs might have when reared in the sweet and sour stench of wet and filthy conditions.

Soon the concrete base of their improved quarters was completely dried out, they had ample bedding to replace their mother's warmth and a correct balanced near-liquid diet was available in lieu of the buttons along her nutritional milk bar. After each meal time they would go back to their bedding and sleep, lying close together, side by side like sardines. I would always make sure that their trough was quite empty, for foodstuff left to go stale can cause trouble. On one occasion however, I looked into the empty trough and there, at the bottom was my own wristlet watch, of considerable sentimental value. (My dear wife was not amused.)

Given the opportunity, a pig will churn up soil with its nose to gain quite a lot of nourishment from roots and it was my intention to allow them freedom in the paddock at the rear of the house as soon as they were a little older.

The fencing had by now proved itself capable of containing sheep and had even withstood the escape attempts of goats, but before turning the pigs loose all the wire netting would have to be pegged firmly to the ground, for five little snouts would very soon attempt to lift it up and wriggle out from beneath.

Pigs will graze quite well on pasture, providing they have rings pierced through their noses, to cause discomfort if they attempt to root up the turf, so as I had already got rid of the brambles, and the goats had eaten most of the nettles and thistles, my theory was that if the pigs were turned loose unringed they could not only enjoy the grass that was available, they could also help themselves to the bramble roots and anything else they found edible in the ground. The land would be roughly rotovated and manured, the hens would enjoy a selection of worms and insects, then, if I sent the pigs off to market, fastened in the hens, scattered a layer of grass seed I could sit back and see what happened.

The rooting procedure was controlled within separate areas by using an electric fence, and by throwing down handfuls of pig nuts in strategic positions the activity could be concentrated exactly where needed. Although these electric fencing units will work off an old car battery, the shock they give over a short distance is quite awakening. If the thing is making a "ticking noise", it's working, but somewhere along the line there might be a twig from a hedge just touching it, enough to run all the current down to earth, so the best way to carry out a test is to walk along to the furthest point, take a blade of grass and hold it onto the wire. A spasmodic tingle will tell you that all your insulators are in order and the contraption is functioning. No wonder a little pig will jump back smartly if it happens to make contact with a wet nose while standing on damp grass!

The pigs were always fastened inside the building at night-time and their freedom during the day was only at my discretion, for it would not have been good for them to lie out in sunshine and get burnt. They soon grew into strong healthy, firm youngsters with their vigorous outdoor activities, a fact that was to become very noticeable later on, for sitting at a table one certainly can tell the difference between an animal that is all firm muscular flesh from an energetic free range existence, and one that has been fattened in a sty on gallons of pig swill.

One day we arrived back from working on the Quayside and found that the pigs were missing, all five of them. We searched around and then spotted the little group trotting along beside a hedge on the far side of a neighbour's field. I called out aloud, banged a bucket, and they all came running home like very obedient children, but later that evening the phone rang and I learnt my children had been very naughty – they'd been digging holes in somebody's lawn.

They were getting bigger and more boisterous every day, the enthusiastic squealing every feed time was getting louder and louder. To get into the building each morning with their first meal of the day I had to throw some turnips or raw potatoes to the far side of the floor then quickly fill the troughs before they came rushing back towards me. Those old insanitary pigsties in the farmyard at least gave the advantage of being able to feed without walking inside and being knocked over by the animals.

They began to hurl themselves at the wooden door whenever they heard me coming, I expected it to splinter any day, their time had come, they were big enough to send to Douglas.

A cattle wagon backed into the farmyard, the driver lowered the ramp at the rear, then, carrying an empty bucket I led my protégés inside, each receiving a slap on the backside with a multi-needled tattoing instrument, giving them an identification number for the life hereafter as they entered.

The ramp rose, the doors closed, and five little piggies went to market.

CHAPTER 22

THE MARKET

EVERYTHING was working out wonderfully well in our new life, the farm house renovation had even surpassed our most ambitious dreams. The months spent in the tiny cottage in Ramsey had been very happy and all the improvements we had carried out there were reflected in the subsequent sale price that had become a deposit on the old waterfront warehouse.

Within a short space of time we'd acquired not only a country homestead, but also made a satisfactory start in a commercial venture, everything was going so well, every minute was to be enjoyed, how could we be so lucky?

Inside our "Market" premises I'd erected stalls and fitted shelving all round the walls, for we had decided that clothing was definitely to be our principal line and to arouse the interest of the general public they must be shown a substantial selection of stock to choose from.

We made single day expeditions by air to England, where, in the space of a few hours, we would commit ourselves to considerable quantities of stock orders.

Fay carried out the selection of every garment, specifying the sizes, colours and quantities required. "Spending money as if it's going out of fashion", she used to say. But I was always alongside calculating potential selling prices and keeping a careful record of the overall expenditure involved as it deepened our commitment to the Isle of Man Bank.

Large mirrors from old wardrobes were sited in strategic parts of the building to create an illusion of greater size and initially all the large cardboard cartons in which the stock had arrived, were emptied and then lifted onto wooden racks on display, adding to the impression of a well-stocked establishment.

Later, as we established a good reputation with various manufacturers and importers we took advantage of the general credit procedure within the textile industry whereby goods purchased up to the nineteenth of a month would require to be paid for on the tenth of the following month, say three weeks grace. But by purchasing very heavily on invoices dated at the beginning of the period (the twentieth of the month) no cash would be required for an additional month, giving seven weeks in which to sell as much as possible before signing a cheque.

A certain amount of elementary book-keeping is essential even in the most straightforward of businesses, to differentiate between the profits and the losses and ensure that an overall progress is being maintained. My life had certainly covered a variety of activities and a little useful knowledge had been picked up here and there, but as far as paperwork was concerned I think the three years spent as a junior bank clerk, though hardly exciting, were now standing me in good stead.

My personal attempts to sell items of clothing direct to the customer were absolutely pathetic, I mumbled, hesitated, felt embarrassed and lost patience, thank goodness the same limitation didn't apply to Fay. On the contrary, she had all the charm and chatter of an ideal saleslady, she gained a lot of satisfaction and was an absolute inspiration to the girls and ladies who later joined us. We formed a satisfactory combination based loosely on the words, "You sell the tickets Love, I'll drive the bus".

Many customers needed privacy to try the various garments for size, so I built a couple of fitting rooms with timber framework and curtaining so that ladies could pop inside and then step out again to ask their husband's opinion about the proposed bargain purchase they were wearing. One afternoon, however, a couple of ladies came into the building, accompanied by a gentleman, the ladies made their way along our rails of merchandise and each selected a dress of their choice, then, to our amazement, all three of them went into a small fitting room and pulled the curtain closed. We still wonder what went on in that fitting room and what on earth sort of relationship existed between the trio, but at least the price of those two dresses certainly contributed nicely to the takings of the day.

We had become quite resigned to the necessity of keeping our premises open each day during the summer season running our Toy-Town Market, carrying out only the bare essentials of our rural lifestyle until later in the year. We must have been very naive in those early days, for it was only when I found skirt hangers hidden behind mirrors did I realise that in spite of there being such a happy, easy-going welcome given to everyone, there were some people stealing our stock. A skirt was inconspicuous when leaving the premises worn under a dress, but the hanger it came off had to be disposed of.

I rigged up a small electric buzzer so we could signal to each other across the floor area. Whenever Fay spotted anybody acting suspiciously I would sally forth to do my "heavy breathing" performance. This was a non-talking part I played quite well, by simply standing very close to the suspect and following him or her round from stall to stall, until they left the building either with a guilty conscience or maybe the disapproval of my specific brand of soap.

Providing the weather was fine it was a delightful position in which to be employed, through the wide open double doorway was an array of pleasure craft and fishing boats in the harbour and one only had to step across the roadway with a few scraps of food and the seagulls would swoop down from the swing bridge ready to catch individual morsels in mid-air as they left your hand.

Young Tony toddled round from one form of mischief to another, an additional anxiety that was certainly not conducive to general business efficiency. On one occasion a lorry driver ran his front wheels near to a cardboard box by the doorway. It moved, fell on one side and out rolled our little fellow.

The schoolgirls would sometimes take turns to walk him round the town and I well remember taking him myself for a little fresh air and exercise in the park. We made our way slowly towards the swings and I quite quickly noticed that the only other people in the vicinity were a tiny little girl, about Tony's age, and a very attractive young woman to whom she was responsible.

Half an hour of my baby minding duties passed very pleasantly as I sat on a swing, gentle easing myself to and fro in conversation with such a delightful personality, while our respective children played nearby. I felt rather deflated however when it was time to leave and the charming voice was directed towards Tony saying "Bye, Bye now, ask Grandad to bring you again sometime".

CHAPTER 23

END OF SEASON

ALTHOUGH so happy and satisfied with the new life of our choice we nevertheless had many lingering thoughts for the relatives and friends who, at one time we took so much for granted, when they were only motoring distance away, and would now be pleased to see more regularly, but any such visit now involved an expensive air ticket or a day spent crossing the water, plus complicated arrangements for the attendance to livestock if the pair of us were to be absent for more than just a few hours.

The highlights of our off-shore mode of living were without doubt the eagerly anticipated visits of "our boys", this being a collective term we were pleased to use without referring to the dismal complications of earlier heartbreaks, for the three sons we boasted of were in reality, his, hers, and ours.

My own son Roger was at University and I'd met the colleagues with whom he shared accommodation, together with the kindly landlady who considered that each of her young men should always start the day with a mountain of baked beans on toast.

His summer visits sometimes involved the loan of the family car and time spent swimming and sunbathing at Laxey, or water skiing across Douglas Bay but he was well aware that success in his immediate studies would have a very crucial effect upon his whole future.

Fay's son Malcolm was a little younger and had just started an insurance career in Manchester where he lodged with one of his mother's sisters. He very much wanted to drive a car and had been able to take advantage of the Manx law which allows youngsters to use "L" plates and take a steering wheel at the tender age of sixteen.

Shortly after we had sailed across, one very revered old personality had peacefully passed away from the family circle, my own grandmother Teare. Just a frail little lady whose joy of reading had widened her knowledge far beyond the confines of the Isle of Man and England. She could also speak in considerable detail of her childhood days when half a cup of milk per week and a small piece of meat once a month were family luxuries, but this remarkable little soul kept mobile and mentally alert right up to her one-hundred-and-sixth year.

The Ballaneddin kitchen layout, large pantry and wine store, with livestock, fishfood and fresh vegetables so readily at hand, coupled with Fay's excellent cooking ability and my own healthy appetite meant that many wonderful evenings were spent at the table in Henry the Eighth style, with a tankard in one fist and a big bone in the other.

We both enjoyed big savoury meals so very much but we needed to bear in mind the sinister consequences of too many calories, and too much cholesterol. I'm not sure what Henry had too much of, but he didn't even reach my age. We didn't eat the wrong foods, but on many occasions I think we ate too much of the right ones and it was a rather sobering thought to recall one of old Grandma's questions to me as a little boy: "do you eat to live, or do you live to eat?"

Tremendous satisfaction is gained when entertaining friends at a table full of culinary creations that have been home produced but we also enjoyed an additional bonus when we dined on certain items that were growing wild and freely available for anyone to collect. One vegetable example of this was spinach, we knew where an abundance of a very palatable mild flavoured variety grew close to the water's edge, we could pick the youngest and most tender leaves all through the summer, and store some in the freezer for other times, finding it more popular than the garden variety.

Mushrooms were generally quite plentiful at the right time of the year, it was just a matter of knowing where to look and having the time to collect them. Most years a few really big ones, as big as saucers, would appear right inside the farm yard overnight and were delicious when picked up, and fried straight away with a couple of rashers of bacon, before the goats wandered over them.

Many other types of fungus make an appearance with the warmth of the spring or the moisture of the autumn in various shapes, sizes and colours. Some are delicious, some are tasteless and some are very poisonous. So for any inexperienced collector, a botanical reference book with plenty of colourful illustrations is an absolute necessity. Even so, if there is ever the slightest doubt about the identification of any fungus that is to be considered for eating, it must be thrown away immediately.

I've certainly enjoyed plenty of the ink caps, for every year they popped up through the loose stones of the driveway outside our front door, they need to be collected when very young, cooked and eaten straight away, for if you leave them in the kitchen for a few hours you will find that your delicacies have become reduced to a mushy, inky black, liquid. My reference book says that they must never be consumed at the same time as alcohol; dare I say that it sounds like a warning not to drive under the "affluence of inkahol"!

Once I brought home some large, very succulent-looking fungi specimens, with clean white, gilled undersides but smooth dark coloured tops. Looking through my mushroom book I was already anticipating the flavour of something different until I reached a beautiful, full page colour plate of the identical growth to the ones I had earlier found growing in a carpet of oak leaves. The caption below it read "There are many colour forms of the lethal DEATH CAP, which may make it difficult for the beginner to identify".

Without any further hesitation I picked them up and threw them straight into the burning stove and washed my hands.

There was so much interesting information to be learnt about the countryside but just not enough hours in each day to do all the things I would so much like to.

The commercial project on the quayside was so very necessary but unfortunately it was occupying all the best weeks for outdoor activities. Apart from carrying out the administration duties, my time was fiilled entirely with tidying stock, cleaning windows, sweeping the floor, making out tickets, undoing parcels and all the routine chores of a general warehouseman, but all the time keeping a watchful eye for misdemeanours.

Working the seven days of a week, without even a lunch break, becomes rather tedious when it runs on from one month to another and a concrete floor is inclined to make one's legs ache much more by being confined to movements within a small area than it would during a ramble over the hills.

Eventually our first experience of seaside trading in a holiday season was over and we could look back with satisfaction. We'd gained experience, learnt a lot and made very many friendly acquaintances who might have initially come in out of curiosity, but who would now come in at least once a week because they found our market was a good place to call in just for a chat and to exchange a joke.

One hilarious happening of the summer had been the day when the place was full of people and our baby son happened to notice that a lady's bare toes could be seen beneath the fitting room curtain, they were painted bright red and at the time he HAPPENED TO HAVE A LITTLE TOY HAMMER IN HIS HAND!

Had the amount of time at work been totalised we would not have had a particularly good hourly return but we enjoyed the satisfaction of being self-employed. Any serious illness or accident to the pair of us and in a short space of time we would have no business and would subsequently lose our beloved Balla-neddin. Success in a small business sometimes brings envy, and for failure there is usually little sympathy, but it was a wonderful feeling to close those doors at the end of the season and know that we would be only standing on that concrete floor for Fridays and Saturdays until next summer. THAT COULDN'T BE BAD, COULD IT?

CHAPTER 23

CHARLIE DRAKE

HALF a dozen Muscovy ducks and a drake proved to have been a very good purchase indeed, they were big colourful birds, black and white with yellow legs and bright red faces. Not a breed that is regarded as being prolific egg producers, but they do grow to good sized carcases. All ducks need a constant water supply, though not necessarily for swimming in and as our baby had now outgrown his oval-shaped, pale blue plastic bath this was set into the earth in the farmyard and a rainwater downspout led into it. This became immediately popular, particularly with the big drake. Instead of just waddling aimlessly around in an overweight, ungainly manner, he quickly seized upon the opportunity to use the water bath as an exquisite matrimonial bedchamber.

The first eggs to be laid seemed to be produced in a very haphazard manner, just dropped at random in muddy patches here and there giving an atmosphere of "Surprise, surprise, I didn't even know I was expecting".

The shells of these dirty, greyish coloured eggs were much tougher and thicker than the normal hen's eggs and being slightly porous it was advisable to use them only as hard-boiled or for baking purposes.

When the weather became warmer the ducks settled down to the serious matter of reproduction, each one selecting a hiding place either in a hedge bottom or some dark corner of a disused outbuilding and only by deliberate searching did I find these rather primitive "nests" with maybe two or three eggs laying there, but as the days went by the number would increase to ten or even a dozen before each bird would determine that the time had come to start the tedious vigil of hatching her offspring.

Most incubation is carried out artificially nowadays but these ducks of mine didn't know anything whatsoever about elaborate heating apparatus, ventilation requirements, humidity levels, disinfection, fumigation and so on. The broody ducks just sat there, with their feathers all ruffled up to completely cover the eggs, each of which she would roll over several times in a day, ensuring that the embryo didn't adhere to the shell membrane. Within a month a remarkable phenomenon of nature would have taken place whereby a raw egg had been transformed into a fluffy little duckling.

Theoretically there were going to be dozens of these little creatures at Ballaneddin, but one mustn't count ducklings when they're only eggs and it gave us tremendous pleasure when at last the first batch of baby Muscovies had hatched out and the proud mother paraded them in the farmyard. Two eggs still remained in the foot of the hedge, already cold, one contained an evil smelling liquid and went Pop! when I broke it open, the other had a perfectly formed little bird that had just not managed to summon up sufficient strength to break out into the world.

Day by day the flock increased but this was the time that so many predators had been awaiting. The long-tails had been exterminated but there were plenty of polecats in the vicinity and when the number of chicks began to diminish even the behaviour of our tail-less pussy cat came under investigation. Certainly the old bulldog was beyond suspicion for whenever she wandered into the farmyard she seemed to receive a peck on the nose and would promptly turn around and go straight back inside the house. One day, however, I was leaning on the gate quietly admiring the little families as they wandered to and fro in little lines astern amongst the grass, when there was a flutter of black and white feathers as a magpie plunged down from above and scooped up a duckling right before my eyes.

The water bath was quite an attraction and the mothers would watch the little balls of fluff paddling their way across the surface, but as they grew older and bolder, venturing into the water beyond mother's watchful eye, a couple of them drowned. This was rather puzzling at first and the eventual explanation was that the depth of the water varied according to the rain fall and how much of it was splashed over the sides by the adult birds plunging in, consequently if the little ones happened to enter the bath when the water surface was two or three inches below the smooth plastic rim they were unable to climb out again and would eventually be overcome with exhaustion. This problem was soon rectified by putting a large stone inside the bath and against the side, offering them a means of exit.

Rearing agricultural livestock can be very satisfying, there is an immense pleasure to be gained from watching your own young birds or animals develop into good healthy mature specimens but there must always be a careful consideration of the cost relationship of each egg, each pint of milk or each ounce of flesh against the value of foodstuff consumed, a food conversion ratio.

We had some laying hens, the word laying and its continuance being the sole reason for their existence and a non-productive bird, or even one whose performance was below that of her sisters, was only growing older, tougher and of less value. Generally a defaulter could be noticed by having a smaller and less healthy looking comb but to chase it round the building and grab hold of it would cause so much noise and alarm that some of the others could be put off-lay for a day. The simplest approach was to go along the perches after dark with an electric torch, calmly take hold of the bird required, lift it down without any fuss or flutter and gently feel the distance between the pelvic bones. If an egg was being passed through there at daily intervals the space between the bones would be about the width of three fingers. Two fingers or less meant a quiet withdrawal from the building and a quick dislocation of the bird's head from the top of its neck causing instantaneous death, although there could be the nervous flailing of wings in the air for two or three minutes.

Blood drains into a gap immediately behind the skull where the skin of the neck has been extended, so, for our own household use no further bleeding was required. The killing and plucking procedures were normally carried out as one operation, for the feathers are loosest before the body cools. I've seen some people push a knife up through the roof of the unfortunate bird's mouth into the brain, this is said to release the feathers and carry out bleeding at the same tinme. A gruesome procedure, not recommended for the squeamish.

Many people who have idealistic dreams of a self-sufficient lifestyle and long to collect their own warm freshly laid eggs from the nests of contentedly clucking hens would shudder at some of the unpleasantries involved. The "necking" of poultry is quick and humane and with a certain amount of self-discipline can be undertaken as being a recognised necessity but if a quantity of old stock has been dispatched and then the same amount of strength applied to stretch a smaller, younger bird, it can result in the horrific awareness of holding a detached head in one hand and becoming blood spattered by a writhing, decapitated corpse in the other.

Eventually the ducklings reached a weight that was acceptable to the local butcher and beyond which would have involved the purchase of much more poultry meal; they were all shut up for twenty-four hours in the disused shippen with a supply of water but no food. This starvation ensures an empty crop and reduces the amount of material in the intestines. Unless this is done there is likely to be a rather unappetising gangreneish green area of flesh around the abdomen caused by the decomposition of food inside the digestive tract.

The plucking of ducks is a little more time-consuming than dealing with chickens for there's a layer of "down" beneath the feathers. Because of the quantity of birds involved it was worth my while to pay for the plucking to be carried out by machine on the basis of an agreed price per carcase.

The ducks were that much larger and stronger than the chickens I had dealt with so easily, and with such an extra length on neck it was better for me to hold the bird's head downwards to the floor, place an iron bar across the back of its neck, speedily put my toes down on the bar and jerk upwards to give that instantaneous dislocation.

The butcher was very pleased with the neatly plucked and dressed young ducks he purchased, Fay was delighted to have a quantity for our own use inside the deep freeze and although the farmyard now seemed so much quieter, the adult birds stayed close to Charlie Drake as he eyed the bath tub. For them, there would be another mating season.

CHAPTER 25

LA CUISINE

WE had razor sharp knives and a bone saw at the ready to deal with the carcases that were brought into the kitchen from the abattoir but very soon found that, for a pair of amateurs, a modern kitchen table is a very flimsy and unsafe substitute for a butcher's workbench. So to reduce the possibility of any fingers dropping in the pie we arranged for a joiner-made table to be produced of thick pine wood to our specific requirements, of quite presentable appearance for general use but sufficiently robust to withstand a much heavier onslaught when necessary.

The first joints of meat produced looked rather ragged specimens, not exactly supermarket display pieces and later on when they came out of the deep freeze for use were found to be generally bigger than would normally be purchased for our small household. No meat was wasted but this started a tendency to eat much larger portions, simply because they were at hand. This was not good for either figure or fortune.

More experience was gained with the passing of time for we were soon butchering four lambs a year, plus an occasional pig, so the dismembering of each carcass was carried out with reasonable speed and efficiency. Sometimes we ate hogget, this is the name given to a lamb when it becomes over one year old, making it less tender but carrying more flavour. It is certainly a great advantage for the cook to know the fullest background details of the raw material that is to be used.

Sheeps' head broth is becoming just a childhood memory in our affluent society, probably the skinning of a skull is now regarded as being too time consuming but in other European countries even such lowly morsels as chicken's heads and chicken's feet are offered in the shops. A much more interesting headpiece is of course that of a pig which is so easily absorbed into the traditional recipe incorporating ear'oles, eye'oles, nose'oles and what-have-you to make delicious brawn. Unless most of the fat is skimmed off in the course of cooling however, this can turn out to be a little too rich for some palates but at Ballaneddin such greasy surplus became baked with oatmeal and other kitchen scraps to re-emerge as very acceptable home-made dog biscuits.

Fay's large oblong shaped pork pies, with a row of eggs lying down the middle were always popular, but it wasn't till I saw them being made that there was the obvious realisation that the eggs had to all be hardboiled before being placed into position with the meat.

Some of her tastiest dishes were made with a meat content that would have only cost a few coppers even from a shop, for example strips of belly pork marinated for about twenty-four hours in soya sauce, sugar, dry sherry and garlic were, in my opinion anyhow, absolutely delicious.

When our week-long stints inside the Quayside Market reached their conclusion, there were still plenty of sunny days at the beginning of September to be enjoyed and one of the easiest forms of mental relaxation was to wander round the lanes collecting blackberries. With a container hung round your neck and a twig in one hand to pull the berries towards you for picking off with the other, a quiet productive couple of hours could be spent in fresh air and country solitude that could be recalled with satisfaction months later when sipping blackberry wine.

Once the basic equipment for winemaking has been acquired such as a few fermentation jars, bungs and air locks there's no reason why production shouldn't be carried out all the year round, utilising not only the various fruits as they come into season, but a variety of vegetables — even potatoes and many of the items off the pantry shelf, such as raisins, barley, ginger, and the most commonplace of all, which we have certainly enjoyed, the everyday packet of tea.

Fermenting quietly away in the warmth of the bathroom airing cupboard were usually about ten glass demi-johns each holding about a gallon of liquid going through the process that would result in a selection of wines of varying colours and flavours. My own manly responsibilities in this particular activity were confined to the sampling and corking. Fay would syphon off the liquid into bottles and I would take corks from the boiling water in which they had been not only sterilised but also made pliable, place them individually into a gadget that was merely a wooden funnel with an outlet end that was slightly smaller than the neck of an ordinary wine bottle, then by using a wooden plunger while the cork was still hot, wet, soft and slippery, ram it firmly into position.

Within the cool darkness of the outside pantry, set half-way into the hillside, I'd stacked rows of wooden tomato boxes each with one side broken away to form ideal racking facilities where the bottles, four to a box, should theoreticaly remain unopened for several months or even years, alas the temptation was often too great and many of them never really reached their full maturity.

Certain shortcuts can be taken just by going into a shop and getting a can of mushy grape concentrate, following the instructions on the wrapper and wine can be declared drinkable within a month. This of course involves a little more expenditure, for in the basic do-it-yourself manner a wide range of wines can be produced for little more than the cost of the sugar, and even this item can be reduced by the bulk purchase of hundredweight or fifty kilo sacks, but the ultimate decision must generally depend on the preference of the household and their degree of thirst.

Beer in the ready-to-mix kit forms we found to be much more convenient than boiling up pans full of hops. The end products were of good flavour, clear and quite potent; so much so that with a five gallon container always in the kitchen it was very easy to over-indulge. Many evenings were concluded, after a hard day's work, with a huge savoury meal accompanied by three to four pints of home brew or maybe a litre of wine, a lusty singsong around the kitchen stove and then a precarious ascent up the wooden hills to be in bed and fast asleep before ten o'clock.

Just as the consumption of pork chops and lamb casseroles needed voluntary curtailment so too did the intake of home produced alcohol. We had never lived so well in our lives and it would have been utterly stupid to endanger our health by ending each evening with a bloated stomach and a fuddled brain.

The judicial use of garlic gave Fay's kitchen a distinctly continental atmosphere and many of her presentations bore a very noticeable French influence. I have lived over there at one time and had since then been pleased to introduce my wife to many families, and into the homes of dear friends I had made. We were consequently more conversant with the home cooking of the countryside, rather than the haute-cuisine of the expensive Paris restaurants.

One memorably romantic occasion however we had sat in a café along the bank of the Seine and my dear lady had requested a portion of *les escargots*, not as a connoisseur, but purely as a first time taster. Although I already considered they were both over-rated and over-priced this was a time when I needed to display a genial generosity. Then, here in the Isle of Man some years later, those same confounded species were silently gliding out of the sanctuary of a dry-stone wall each night to chomp their way through my lettuce seedlings and disappear again at dawn before the birds could snatch them.

However, a mischievous thought occurred that they would make a quite unique starter course for our next dinner party, so, by searching under leaves and stones four dozen good sized specimens were collected into a plant pot and left overnight to empty themselves. Although a piece of wood had been placed over the top they must have made a combined effort to escape, for, next morning the wood had been slightly moved and there wasn't a solitary snail in sight.

Perhaps our guests would have considered the incident thankfully, we did however prepare some at a later date, purely for our own entertainment rather than hunger, frying the fleshly pieces that skid along the ground in butter and herbs, then scalding the largest of the empty shells, packing with butter and poking two or three of the shrivelled morsels into each opening, sealing with further butter and giving final decoration with a sprig of parsley. (We never bothered doing it again.)

CHAPTER 26

NOEL

GREENHOUSES usually get stripped of their unripe tomatoes as autumn approaches so that was the time when Fay usually made about fifty pounds of chutney, much of which was always given away to her friends; we'd also learned that if a large green tomato was sliced and given a quick fry on either side in a spot of bacon fat it became quite a pleasantly flavoured vegetable.

The next priority had to be the getting together of ingredients for the Christmas cake and puddings, followed by the traditional stirring and wishing, but unfortunately without the addition of any tiny silver three-penny pieces which are no longer in circulation.

We had now acquired another goat, she was called Penny, an all white gentle creature of the British Saanen breed which seemed to possess all the qualities required to become a good breeder and milk producer. The mating season lasts over the winter, from August to March at intervals of twenty-one days and as soon as she showed the expected symptoms she would need to be taken to see a Billy straight away. Arrangements were made with a breeder only a few miles away that I should pick up the phone to say we were on our way and Billy would be waiting. We had by now obtained a van that was quite big enough to transport goats, pigs, bales of hay and so on, provided it was thoroughly cleansed afterwards, to carry cartons of clothing. We had to hope that Penny's brief forty-eight hour availability would not coincide with the Fridays and Saturdays that had to be spent on the Quayside.

Sure enough, one morning she was not in the least bit interested in a bucket of rolled oats, she just kept up a noisy bleating, an almost continuous switching of her tail and peered over the fence like a captive maiden calling for the attention of a knight in shining armour.

Into the van she jumped with no trouble and at our destination alighted again without hesitation and her future mate was brought forward on a lead. A Billy has a strong goaty smell at the best of times, but in the breeding season this becomes even stronger; he was certainly a pedigree Stinking Billy. He went straight to her head and made some little muttering movements with his lips to which she responded. Then he promptly set about what was his sole purpose in life, soon throwing his head back in an ecstasy climax. Penny could have gone straight back into the van she'd left only minutes earlier. But the lady owner and I chatted for about a further ten minutes, after which he performed once more, with just the same enthusiasm. Nature is wonderful, and it's no use being jealous about these matters.

One evening the phone rang, it was a publican from near Ramsey Harbour saying that a fellow off one of the fishing boats had called in with a heavy parcel for me to collect. This seemed mysterious so I drove along straight away to investigate, the package was certainly there and the instruction had simply been that I should collect, so I opened it up and found many yards of plain white thick quality cloth but there was no clue to its source of origin.

Eventually we were to learn that a friend in England had quantities of this material for disposal and had more or less said to the fisherman, "If you call in the Isle of Man at some time, just put this ashore for Denys Teare". It could come in very handy for a variety of purposes, but its most pleasing use was when I secured a wooden framework along the beams in the ceiling above our bed, fitted curtain rails and Fay was able to drape the material into the form of a *ye olde four-poster bed*. This had been one of the many rainy-day jobs that kept adding little refinements and finishing touches to the general comfort and overall snugness of our Island home, even with a mid-winter gale howling across the Irish Sea we had cosiness and warmth within those thick walls as we relaxed in front of a big wood and peat fire.

Winter is the time when people who have worked for long hours in the summer offering tourist accommodation, can take life easier, providing of course that all their property repairs, painting and decorating, carpet cleaning and so on can be completed to give the spick and span, bright and cheerful seaside holiday image before the first boatload of visitors disembarks in the spring.

The celebration of Christmas seemed to occupy the whole month of December. There were social functions large and small going on throughout the Island every night and I'm sure some folks must have been in a state of semi-exhaustion when it came to the twenty-fourth night of the month.

Although we dined so well throughout the year on home produce it was to be a novelty and a festive treat if we could have a small turkey on the table, for we had not yet ventured into the complicated business of turkey rearing; they're not as hardy as the assortment of birds that thrived around our farmyard.

By the way, did you hear the sad story about the Irish turkey who was looking forward to such a Happy Christmas?

However, behind a public house in the village of St. John's, in the centre of the Island, an annual poultry auction takes place where the producers, who haven't already sold off their birds to butchers shops and their regular customers, bring along the residue and stand with fingers crossed, anxiously watching the drop of the hammer.

We went along with current shop prices firmly in mind, knowing that an estimated difference between live and dead weight would have to be taken into consideration, beyond that we could only look from cage to cage and roughly classify them as light, middle or heavyweight. A sprightly young welter-weight would have served the purpose but we were delighted when, at the end of the day a nod of the head bought two for the price of one, who were scheduled to stand solemnly together in the barn for a few days before going to separate extremes of oven and deep freezer.

Cards came tumbling through the letter box in increasing quantities, bearing conventional rhymes and greetings coupled with a few scribbled words of family news and the good wishes from lifetime friends living far afield. What a pity all this interesting correspondence couldn't be spread throughout the year for there must be a multitude of lonely people way out in the countryside, who wait day by day for the postman to enter their garden gate.

The holly-lined approach to Ballaneddin had become an avenue of crimson berries, this has been said to be a sign of a forthcoming severe winter but can hardly be so, for, although snow falls on high ground, Manx winters are so consistently mild. The birds would, in due course, strip the berries from some of the trees but leave others completely untouched, for, there is apparently a difference in flavour between male and female holly trees and the little birds have their preference.

One day a refuse collecting vehicle turned into the gateway and drove towards the house, I heard the clatter of the emptied bin and then came a knock on the back door.

This, I expected to be a "Happy Christmas" muttered by a

spokesman for the team, who would probably stand there with open hand — the average householder would not wish to incur his wrath for the twelve months that were to come.

Instead, I was very pleasantly surprised to see a smiling face, not wanting any gratuity at all, but with a simple request: "sorry to disturb you, but may I take a couple of snips of your lovely holly, please?"

Amid the commercial trimmings of Christmas a genuine old fashioned goodwill prevails upon the Isle of Man, people say she's behind the times. I HOPE SHE STAYS THAT WAY.

(I don't believe the story of an Islander who was approached in London by a young woman with a proposition concerning cash, whereupon he replied: "no thanks, they do it for apples where I come from".)

CHAPTER 27

FRUIT AND VEGETABLES

THE decorations were still hanging and the unfinished Christmas cake was still in the pantry when the huge summer holiday publicity campaign rolled into motion; newspapers, magazines, television and radio carried tantalising suggestions of where your money should be spent. Thousands of colourful brochures get posted away annually by the Tourist Board, making every endeavour to gain the Island's share of the trade.

Soon the hoteliers are able to count the enquiries they've received and a little later know the number of definite bookings, with deposits they have accepted. So, even by the end of February, they already have a reasonably accurate idea of what the forthcoming season has in store, always providing that there be no disruption of those vital sea and air services to the Island.

The information they gain is invaluable to the many shopkeepers whose stock orders must be geared in ratio to the anticipated holiday arrival figures. Although, with times of inflation and unemployment it does not necessarily mean that the bucket and spade brigade who reach the seaside have a particularly large surplus available for souvenirs, daily ice-creams and the impulsive purchase of eye-catching garments.

Farmers had brought their sheep down to lower ground, soon the new year offsprings were being born and, having previously been so successful we decided to hand-rear five meg lambs. First of all we had to hold each pathetic little creature still, open its mouth, and ensure that some of the food we'd mixed as substitute for mother's milk went down several times a day, until a rubber teat on the end of a bottle became acceptable. They all came on very well and were soon frolicking about like five pretty little baby

Bambis. I was able to make a rack to hold five separate bottles which they would bore into with great enthusiasm and, having struggled to keep the contraption upright, I certainly have pity for any poor old ewe whose back legs get bumped up off the ground time and again by a couple of boisterious youngsters burrowing vigorously at her nipples underneath. Even with all the good will in the world the rearing of motherless lambs still has its complications, three of the little creatures were found dead without the slightest indication of any prior illness, but the survivors were a bonny couple of males who in due course reached the age for castration and the docking of their tails.

Each of these operations is carried out by placing in position a very tight fitting rubber ring, that stops all circulation until the encumbring items shrivel and drop off. The man who sold me the necessary appliance which gives the fittings a four way stretch, before snapping them into position, assured me that the procedure was quite painless. But how did he know?

The winter bareness of the hawthorn hedges began to give way to the first tinges of green foliage, the mornings became lighter and less cold, the crowing rooster had a supporting dawn chorus from some of the other birds, the sparrows, tits, robins, starlings and thrushes who, together with the cooing woodpigeons and the cock pheasant with its croak like a dying gearbox, all had nests to make and eggs to lay.

The garden needed turning over and there were seeds to be planted but a great assistance this year was to be a recently erected greenhouse. It was only a small one, the bolting together of the metal framework and then the clipping into position of the glass panes had only involved a few hours work but it widened the gardening potential considerably. Shortly however, I was to become involved with fruit and vegetables to a far greater degree than I had ever been before.

The matter started when Fay asked a farmer's wife to call into the Quayside market one weekend with a few cauliflowers, "Leave all the leaves on, they'll do for the animnals", she had said. These were duly delivered but as they lay on the floor near the doorway, people admired the fresh produce and wanted to purchase some. This reaction was quite encouraging and we began to give a little thought to the prospect of allocating part of our trading area to the display of green groceries. No definite move was made until we happened to be at one of the friendly dinner parties we so often enjoyed, a gathering of folk who would wine and dine, frequently with emphasis on their own particular produce, in a more homely and more economic style than if we met inside a restaurant. In the course of the evening we were introduced to a potato merchant and his wife. We discussed the various vegetable crops they grew and the marketing potential on the Quayside, which then led to an introduction to a Douglas wholesaler who had a van coming over daily from Liverpool with bananas, oranges and all the items that were not readily available locally. furthermore he would deliver goods to our premises every day.

Aware now that a complete range of produce was so readily obtainable I made alterations to a corner of our trading area that had previously been displaying gents shirts, bought two types of scale, one a seesaw type of potato scale with weights, and the other, more sophisticated, that had a finger giving the reading across a dial that was calibrated into cash ranges. Very soon I was ready to go into action as a sort of non-mobile barrow boy but standing in my own precinct, at least it would seem more workmanlike than folding baby clothes for hour after hour.

Certainly there was a lot to be learnt about the fruit and vegetable trade for up to that time I had been, when necessary, a dutiful but rather naive shopping husband who would simply hand over his wife's list of requirements saying "There you are, put them in a box please, I'll call back later", totally unaware of all the intricacies such as asking where the onions came from, then squeezing every one to test against softness, asking if the oranges have thick or thin skins. "Are they juicy?" "Are they sweet?" "Have you tasted one yourself?" and so on.

This project was to bring me much more into direct contact with the public than before and would necessitate diplomatic tolerance while attending to the whims and wants of my fellow creatures, calling for a shopkeeper's tongue-in-cheek servility.

Over recent years, in order to strengthen its economy, the Manx Government had been encouraging people to come and take up residence upon the Island; following so much political upheaval throughout various parts of the world many white families had been forced to make a move and providing they had been able to get their capital away in time, the Isle of Man had become a very peaceful retirement haven.

These people had slipped quietly into the community and indeed many have a wealth of experience to offer in certain matters, but, having spent a large portion of their lives in some other country, it was understandable that time and again their conversation should start with the expression 'When I was in . . .' Unfortunately in so many cases this occurs with such monotonous regularity that they became referred to locally as the 'When-eyes'.

This is in humour rather than having a derogatory intention, for the Island folk are basically a friendly people who have a good sense of humour and the use of nick-names seems to be more commonplace than elsewhere.

A friendly word with which Manxmen frequently address one another sounds like 'Yusser' and is perhaps derived from the seafaring salutation of 'aye, aye, sir'. The days went by quite merrily in the Quayside Market as the 'Yussers' and the 'When-eyes' came along to make their purchases. Even if some misguided new arrival happened to find out that the fellow who served the fruit and vegetables was a little bit touchy if addressed as if he were a poor underprivileged servant on another continent.

Casual conversation could cover a wide and interesting field amongst people having such a variety of backgrounds. Some would have had world wide experiences and were now delighted to be back home once more in the land of their birth. Others were entirely new residents whose earlier occupations and achievements were completely unknown.

Speculation about personal histories could always pass an idle moment. Suppose a middle-aged couple had purchsed a quite desirable local dwelling but spent much of their time in sunshine of the Mediterranean or even Florida. "Was he really such a highly successful builder?"

"Or is he a bricklayer who has won the football pools and found the sudden wealth to be an embarrassment in his hometown?"

Further speculation could of course incorporate the regrettable statistic that such a vast amount of highly profitable illegal activity goes undetected throughout the world today, but perhaps we'd better dismiss such thoughts, for we knew very well that no-one has ever been seen coming off the I.O.M. boat with crew-cropped hair, a striped jersey and carrying a big sack, clearly marked SWAG over his shoulder.

Anyhow, I've been told that money is like manure . . . DOES MORE GOOD IF IT'S SPREAD ABOUT!

CHAPTER 28

RECLAMATION

PROGRESS at the country dwelling had been satisfactory, though so very time consuming, but all activities were still confined to within the two acres of the immediate vicinity of the house.

The pride of ownership of the further twenty-eight acres was countered by the awareness that it was an utterly unproductive wilderness, in which even the standing timber that we needed for fuel was almost inaccessible. The short lane leading to the foot of our hill was so completely overgrown by the hawthorn hedges, unattended for decades, whose thorny branches now met across the pathway and were densely intermingled with spikey gorse and bramble entanglements to make it virtually impenetrable. On the top of the hill, however, there was a patchwork of dry stone walls dividing the high land into small fields that had been successfuly farmed long before the advent of agricultural tractors. From a distance it was still possible to discern amongst the dense foliage the outline of the trail zigzagging up the steep incline to give access to the ruined fortification that had been built up there a couple of thousand years earlier. Surely with a world food shortage, territory that had once been productive hadn't been lost for ever? The onus was solely upon my shoulders, what could be done about it?

Making contact with the Government's Agricultural Adviser was very simple, he was a jovial fellow who lived nearby. "I'll come along tomorrow afternoon", he had said, without hesitation.

We laid the farm plan out on the kitchen table and then, wearing wellingtons and armed with soil testing equipment, we set off across my neighbour's pasture to reach the edge of the Ballaneddin jungle. Together we scrambled over the first ten acres of steep overgrown hillside, disturbing pheasants and partridge as we stumbled upwards and upwards until, looking back we could see the layout of the village below and follow the ribbon-like country lanes leading towards the coastline. In the far distance, across the blue water, we could see the outline of the mountains of Northern Ireland on our left and the Scottish lowlands to our right, faintly along the horizon. A strong wind was blowing but the sky was clear and the view absolutely magnificent. We paused for a while and took a sample of the soil but my companion was soon ready to stride off further across the summit. His legs were longer, and younger too, and I was already feeling glad that I didn't have to start a day's work building those walls, stone by sone, as Islanders had done so long long ago, they must have been a very hardly little breed indeed.

The friendly expert was very pleased with the several samples he took from the windy gorselands, there was certainly an intial indication that with appropriate fertilisation and cultivation very good quality pasture could be produced up there.

The descent was not so demanding and we stopped frequently to speculate upon the possibility of an earth-moving machine cutting its way into the side of the hill, building up a shoulder of soil and stones on which to proceed foot by foot diagonally upwards thus widening the existing pathway that was in most places merely a sheep track.

This seemed a feasible prospect providing the entire ascent could be carried out in one long straight line but this was not so, the route would have to be in four separate lengths running zig-zag-zig-zag, "How on earth could a driver and his machine, crawling precariously along a steep diagonal zig, turn round to cut his way into a zag going in the opposite direction?" I asked the expert.

"The machine could work going forward and then in reverse, forward then reverse and would be at the top", came the reply, almost making me think that perhaps Hannibal's elephants had been able to climb uphill backwards too.

The outcome of the expedition came into deep consideration when we settled down together back again at the kitchen table with paper, pen and cups of coffee. The voice of experience assured me that a good contractor would be able to make a roadway up to the top of my piece of territory and at least fifteen acres of the dome shaped summit could be brought under cultivation again, the precise area being dependent upon the skill, or maybe the daring, of whoever was going to drive a tractor tilted over at a difficult angle.

The recommended programme was that first of all there should be a great burn off of all the gorse and bracken, this can only be carried out between certain dates because of the preservation of breeding wildlife, then, the charred landscape should be rotovated three times, whereby all the stumps of charcoal and dried roots be smashed up and buried into the soil. Lime was to be applied at a rate of four tons to the acre, a crop of rape and ryegrass to be sown, grown and either eaten off or taken off. The following year there would need to be further rotovation, cultivation, fertilisation and then a final seeding that would produce a permanent pasture.

This was just a straightforward agricultural land reclamation scheme for someone who knew precisely what he was doing but as the estimated costing was jotted down on a sheet of foolscap paper and totalled I began to consider the limitation of my own experience of breeding livestock, for even after the deduction of a Government reclamation grant there was still a considerable amount of outlay involved. Particularly when there was also stock proof fencing to be borne in mind, although this too could be subject to government assistance providing it was carried out with stumps of a minimum size, suitably pickled for preservation, and with netting and barbed wire of a specified gauge.

The information had all been very enlightening, Fay and I were quite delighted to know that those extra acres of our tiny kingdom could become productive once more. We now had a fair idea of how much outlay would be involved, but the unknown factor concerned the amount of return that could be anticipated. This figure would be dependant upon my ability to buy, to rear and to sell off livestock profitably. We took many matters into careful consideration, for, although only a handkerchief sized piece of land to many farmers, the decision was very important in our own household. Could we really take on any further activity when already both our feet were virtually nailed to the Ramsey Quayside all summer?

While still in a state of uncertainty, a local young farmer came into conversation with us. He was eager to gain the use of more land, and after a couple of discussions a legal document was drawn up which seemed to be quite amicable for each party. He was to conduct the reclamation as recommended by the agricultural adviser and in return for his outlay he would have the use of the land for a period of ten years by the simple annual payment to us of four fat lambs. What more could we wish for?

Work soon got under way, with a machine belching diesel exhaust into the country air as it tore a ragged pathway through the lane, to carve a roadway across the face of the hillside. Everything went according to the proposed programme and soon the young farmer was passing through our farmyard each day to drive his tractor up the zig-zag trail to carry out the rotovation and cultivation of the hilltop, but every time I felt concern for his safety. The more land he reclaimed, the greater was the benefit to us both, but tractor work is dangerous when hill farming and one fatality had recently taken place nearby. I was considerably relieved when he finally came down, the operation completed, for in that sort of occupation there can only be a thin demarcation line between hillside and suicide.

CHAPTER 29

FAMILY AFFAIRS

THE most regular of our staying guests at Ballaneddin was Pop, my spritely octogenarian father whose arrival at the airport would always start with a friendly wave as he walked towards the terminal buildings, then a huge smile and a warm handshake as the distance was closed. Invariably there would be a newspaper under one arm and I knew very well that there was a good chance of the crossword having been completely filled in during the flight. I also knew that as soon as he entered the Quayside Market he would start to tactfully point out the various spelling errors, here and there, amongst the dozens of homemade sales slogans displayed around the building. Never would I have convinced him that ladies will buy briefs regardless of whether the "i" comes before the "e" or not and folks buy bananas because the price is right though not necessarily the number of "n"s for, although long retired, he was still the traditional old-time village headmaster.

Well could I remember the days of his whole-hearted enthusiasm as prime organizer of sports days, scouting, garden fêtes, community singing and other activities that had made him the life and soul of the village. There were also more serious memories for in those days everyone with troubles seemed to knock at the door of either the vicarage or the school house, but now he was just a well respected old gentleman who lived alone and pottered around exchanging cheerful reminiscences with anyone who had time to listen.

Tony's other grandfather, Andrew, was a short stockily built gentleman with a very strong Scottish accent, who was utterly delighted to be amongst our livestock whenever he visited the Island. In earlier days he had toiled from dawn to dusk behind a team of horses and loved to be left alone all day, while Fay and I were out at work, to be completely in charge of all the poultry and various animals. One day the pair of us were walking across the farmyard when he pointed to a fifty-six pound weight lying on the ground then bent down and picked it up by curling his little finger through the rusty iron ring on the top. "I used to be able to do this with either hand when I was young Denys", he said, hoisting the half-hundredweight aloft above his head. I don't recall saying anything particularly appropriate about his little performance at the time, but the following day when I happened to be in the yard alone I decided to do the same, but the excruciating pain of rusty metal nearly tearing my finger off changed my mind halfway.

Frequently I would arrive home in the evening and ask if he'd care for a beer in the village. This he always enjoyed, but never on any occasion would he leave the vicinity of the farm without being thoroughly washed, shaved, wearing a collar and tie and with well polished shoes. There was a lot to be learned in both cleanliness and courtesy from those two old grandfathers.

Our two boys over in England had probably been having quite enjoyable bachelor-hoods but when I went across to attend Roger's graduation I was introduced to a charming young lady who was scheduled to become his future wife, and shortly afterwards Malcolm came to the Island for a few days accompanied by an attractive young companion who went back wearing a ring as his fiancée.

We looked forward to the regular visits of my brother and his wife for to them, as teachers, the whole Island seemed like one large playground they could enjoy to the full, without the responsibility of looking after kids. There was always much laughter, leg-pulling and raucous singing to end the day.

Fay's cooking programme was often varied according to the known food preferences of our family visitors, but if at any time she became at a loss to know what to present she could always refer to a list, that was pinned on the pantry wall, of my own particular favourites.

One of these dishes involved the use of squid, a member of the octopus family that frequently came up in the nets around the Manx waters but at that time was being discarded by the fishermen as an unsaleable proposition. Occasionally my fishing friends would save one and I would be handed a slippery mass of tentacles, stained with the inky liquid that the creature had ejected in desperation, using its own unique but unsuccessful form of defence.

Flopped into a sink of cold running water it would gradually be made to look a little more edible, though still not exactly appetising, by having its thin membrane of outer skin completely peeled away to reveal a pure white meaty pouch, inside which was the nearest approach to a bone to be found, in the form of what looked like a piece of almost transparent, very pliable plastic. The tentacles can also be eaten but this probably depends upon how the fish has been received. If it had been purchased in a shop with hard earned cash I would no doubt prefer to eat the lot but if it had just been thrown ashore as a gift — "Do you want another one next trip?" — then the dog or the cats could enjoy the delicacy of portions that once had wriggled.

The simplest preparation is to cut the envelope into thin strips and fry in butter with seasoning, but this will turn out to be as tough as rubber unless it is previously well pulverised by a purposeful beating with a mallet. After a couple of years using muscle power Fay happened to learn that exactly the same result can be gained by cooking inside a pressure cooker. The end result is certainly very acceptable, whether it be served hot with vegetables or, as in Spain within a salad.

There was a story around the quayside at one time about a fishing boat being tied up and hosed down for the day when the sailor saw a squid lying on the deck, it was still just alive, so he picked it up and took it home to his wife wrapped in newspaper, saying "Here's that sick squid I owed you".

Each summer, amongst the thousands who holidayed upon the Island there were bound to be people who had known Fay and I in earlier years and would make a specific visit to Ramsey with the knowledge that we could be found along the quayside. We were so delighted to see old familiar faces again and hear all the up-to-date information of happenings across the water, but unfortunately it was the busiest time of our year and all the selling of ice-cream, weighing of potatoes and activity amongst the knitwear was our way of earning the bread and butter for the rest of the year. So often our friends would wait patiently for half an hour of their precious sunny holiday time just for a snatch of conversation, but perhaps the bustle of business would only subside as soon as they'd gone away.

Tony soon grew from toddler to a little school boy who spent much of his summer-time contentedly fishing for baby crabs from the swing bridge. One day, at the height of the season, throngs of people were parading along the harbour side, when, looking through the "take-away" opening of my refreshment kiosk I realised that the general movement of pedestrian traffic had partially stopped. Some happening further along the quay was holding their interest, people were in line all looking down into the water.

Fay must have looked up just in time to see about half a dozen customers get scattered aside as I barged out through the doorway, for behind me I heard her screech with motherly intuition "It's TONY!".

Charging madly across the roadway came her pathetic cries from close behind "Oh my baby, Oh my baby!"

Sure enough, our little lad was in the harbour, he'd been climbing across from one fishing boat to another and slipped down in between. The tide was partly out and when we reached the spot a lady had already climbed down the iron rungs of a ladder set into the stone face of the harbour wall, had run along the deck of one of the boats and was struggling to pull the dripping cherub into the safety of the vessel.

While tears gushed profusely between terrified child and palpitating Mummy, the lady to whom we were so very much indebted had quietly left the scene. The pool of water on the harbour's edge and the stream of drips that led across to the market soon dried away in the warmth of the sunshine and the Ramsey waterfront went back again to its more normal tranquillity.

CHAPTER 30

FOOD FOR THOUGHT

THE thick stone walls of Ballaneddin gave each room in the house deep windowsills on which were displayed a choice selection of china and brassware items that blended pleasantly with the rural charm. A couple of oil lamps found in the barn had cleaned up beautifully. Wicks and glass chimneys had been still obtainable from a local hardware shop so they had become not only decorative but also readily available for any emergency use.

One particularly dark winter evening, with a raging gale outside, the house suddenly fell into total darkness.The power supply had been disrupted, the television was off and even the refrigerator had stopped purring. But the couple of hours of absolute tranquillity that were to follow became a period of wonderful nostalgia as we sat together in the subdued lighting, thoughtfully savouring the faint, not unpleasant aroma of the peat burning in the open grate and watching the flickering shadow patterns along the exposed beams of the ceiling where various curiosities and tools of bygone days were hanging.

Speaking softly to each other we enjoyed the simple background rhythm of the slowly ticking clock, appreciating the comfortable warmth and knowing that all our livestock were safely bedded down till morning. We spoke of the less fortunate people on the sea, riding out the storm and were thankful that none of our kinfolk were amongst them.

When the flow of current returned to the electric light bulbs the instant harshness shattered our fireside contentment, giving an immediate desire to switch off and stay within that peaceful atmosphere of the past, but straightaway a stranger's voice violated our privacy as he peered into the room from his magic box to give the nine o'clock news.

International affairs had become a greater source of interest to me in recent years and many early hours of the morning were spent listening to radio news reports and noticing the variations to details of a particular happening as broadcast from different countries of the world.

It was also quite unique to live on a tiny little Island with its long standing Parliament, whose members are voted into office every five years for their basic common sense and honesty, then to consider the political antics going on just across the water.

The Island certainly has strong ties with Britain and bears allegiance to the English crown, cenotaphs stand in silent tribute to the courage and sacrifices of the Manx nation earlier this century. Some people will very well remember when the passenger boats had their white superstructure and cherry red funnels daubed all over with mournful shades of grey in jagged camouflage patterns and the remoseless bombing and shelling they received before sinking into the waters of Calais and Dunkirk in 1940 but sadly, there must now be very few of that earlier generation who can recall when all eight vessels of the I.O.M. Steamship Company with their gallant crew sailed into World War One. Everyone of them was sunk!

In those two major conflicts the Island gave a very high per capita contribution. This was done proudly in the name of 'PATRIOTISM' but in recent years, when watching programmes and hearing broadcasts from the United Kingdom where so many people are demanding more and more money, regardless of the economic consequences, I wonder what the future holds.

However, that's a political matter, one of the many subjects that I know so little about, but one thing is certain, never a day goes by without a Manxman somewhere or other proclaiming with pride the land of his birth.

So many people across the water regard their Member of Parliament as someone who comes from London to walk along the streets wearing a brightly coloured rosette once every five years, but members of the Manx Parliament, the House of Keys, all live amongst the people they represent and have a personal interest in the welfare of every household within their constituency. Contact with one's member is not made through any party headquarters or via a personal secretary, no, you can either pick up the phone or simply go along the road and knock on his front door. Although it is more discreet to ensure that he's neither starting breakfast nor finishing supper at that particular time.

The encouragement of new residents policy had certainly helped the Island's economy but this was unfortunately followed by an era when property and land was snatched up by developers and speculators. Owners did not realise what rapid price increases were taking place. Maybe their own particular domestic circumstances required a speedy transaction, consequently farmlands were being relinquished and there was no legislation whatsoever to stop these large areas of Manx heritage being offered for sale in London the following day at twice the price.

The Isle of Man had become what developers call "An opportunity area, with a potential to be exploited in terms of high finance". This was very disturbing for in a short space of time it could be virtually carved apart by international financiers and even lose for ever the image it so cherished.

The murmurings of discontent began to appear in print as mysterious clandestine news-sheets fell through letter boxes, which, over a period of time, developed into very hard-hitting, grimly humorous publications complete with cartoons revealing a remarkable degree of inside information of the wheeling and dealing that was allegedly taking place in shares, in companies, in land and in properties. The paper's anonymity meant that its accuracy could not be challenged but it was certainly a strong indication of unrest within an apparently well-informed section of the community.

The lighting and carrying of a "fiery cross" had been for many centuries the recognised means of relaying a message of danger through the villages, calling upon clansmen to unite and fight, so I found it quite disturbing to see in the distance a sinister signal high on a hillside, probably created by one match and one can of petrol, portraying for many miles around that all was not well upon the Island. Thank goodness its inhabitants were quite capable of sorting out their affairs without resorting to blood-shed!

There is an official procedure whereby any person who considers they have a grievance is fully entitled to lay a complaint before the Governor, who represents the Queen of England, Lord of Mann, at the annual open air Tynwald ceremony. This right was recently utilised in a matter concerning crime and punishment on the Island, for, though so thankfully the barbaric days of hangings and floggings for trivial offences are all in the distant past, the Courts still had authority to order that a youth proven guilty of causing bodily harm to another human being should receive a specific number of painful whacks across his buttocks with a handful of twigs from the birch tree.

This seemed to be a very elementary and inexpensive form of

administering justice and the courts had very seldom cause to call upon its administration. Crimes of violence were almost non-existent. Since the Island became involved with the European Community, however, and its precise involvement seems a very complicated issue indeed, the member countries (who suffer a much higher incidence of violence) have decreed at Strasburg that the Manx form of punishment is too degrading for the recipient and should be discontinued.

The plea presented to Tynwald was that the Island's own punishment system be retained but it would appear at the moment to be outweighed by an international wave of thought giving greater attention to the welfare of the occasional thug rather than to the sufferings of his unfortunate victims.

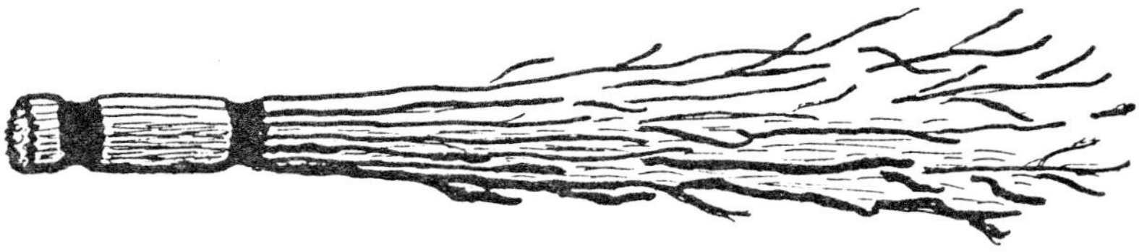

CHAPTER 31

FUNNY BUNNY

MOST town-dwellers can switch off their electrical and gas appliances at night then retire to bed with very little worry about any potential fire danger within their home. Tragedies certainly do take place but in the vast majority of cases the early smell of smoke is detected by some passer-by or a patrolling policeman, the alarm is raised and within one minute of receiving the call at the fire station a well equipped machine will be speeding along to the given address, fully manned with night-shift fire-fighting personnel.

The country cousin is however in a much more vulnerable situation, living within the proximity of many combustible hazards such as spare cans of petrol, paraffin, oil tanks, stores of firewood, bales of hay and straw, plus open fireplaces and solid fuel cooking stoves, but blissfully unconcerned that, should an emergency arise, the nearest fire-fighting crew can all be asleep in their respective homes, resting from their individual daytime occupations.

I had made an experimental contraption whereby certain foodstuffs could be dried quickly and cleanly by utilising the flow of warm air arising from the old solid Sally kitchen stove. This proved to be so successful that it was brought into immediate use for preserving mint, parsley, chopped chives and other herbs in a manner that not only retained the full flavour and green colouring but would continue to do so, providing the storage jars were kept away from direct sunlight. Indeed a considerable improvement on the greyish, dust-collecting bundles that had previously been hung from the beams across the ceiling.

One day the apparatus was filled with greenery and left in the drying position over the stove while we went out for the afternoon but unfortunately the air intake on the stove had not been closed before we left, the top cooking plate had got hotter and hotter, so much so that when we returned the kitchen was full of smoke and the drying unit completely burnt out.

Shortly afterwards a couple of chemical fire-extinguishers were purchased and placed in strategic positions for we were both aware that even after making a frantic 999 call, precious time could elapse and our home become a smouldering ruin.

A Mark 2 drying unit was duly created, from a discarded old all-metal meat safe, which proved to be better, more efficient and with a wider range of usage. Chunks of banana could be dehydrated to resemble hard well-flavoured caramels, slices of apple became leathery little pieces that could be taken from jars and chewed as toffees throughout the year, successful for their novelty value rather than for any dire economic necessity, eventually falling from favour and the interest being replaced by the melting down of quantities of cooking chocolate and utilising a selection of everyday pantry contents, such as currents, raisins, cherries, cornflakes and so on to make our own selection of home-made chocolates. Fiddling around in the kitchen can be good fun, providing that all the mess is cleared up before it is time for the next meal to be prepared.

Improvements to our modernised homestead were continually being made, a hole cut through the floor of the bathroom airing cupboard with a mail-bag suspended in the boiler house below now constituted a very useful laundry-shute; large stones that had previously been lying untidily around were now forming a vehicular roundabout at the end of the drive that was filled with rose bushes, sadly fated to receive a vicious pruning whenever the wretched goats escaped. The roses could understandably be regarded as a succulent part of their balanced diet, but why on earth did those same creatures chew away at the electrical wiring on my tractor?

Although timber for fuel was readily available much time and energy was involved so a policy of heat conservation was gradually carried out. The old worm eaten roller blinds of parchment that had been torn down from the windows and burnt, were replaced with neatly fitting ones of linen. Very efficient in wintertime when pulled down into position and then heavy curtaining drawn across. A secondary door at the rear of the house had not been replaced but we were soon to realise that without it the prevailing wind swept straight into the house whenever one trudged into the rear porch to take off muddy footwear. Originally there had also been a door at the foot of the stairs which had effectively isolated the upper rooms of the house during the daytime, but presumably would have been left open at night for the heat from the fire and cooking stove to rise, not a bad idea really but rarely seen in modern homes.

Many bits and pieces found around the farm were hardly *objets d'art* but were far too interesting to be thrown away. There were out-dated hand tools, gin traps, wrought iron fittings and quite an intriguing block of wood into which had been bored four separate holes large enough for mice to enter. Each mouse could easily reach the bait inside by nibbling its way through a strand of cotton that was stretched tautly across the opening. That was Micky Mouse's good news. The bad news was that, as soon as the strand of cotton parted, a spring wire broke his neck.

Pottering around the outbuildings amongst the livestock was very relaxing and enjoyable and it was easy to become so involved with the particular task in hand that all track of time was completely lost. Inside the house however we kept a school hand-bell for Fay to step outside and wang up and down calling me in from playtime, to a meal on the table, or maybe to a voice on the telephone. Across the field we would sometimes hear the shrill blast of a referee's whistle signifying a similar message being sent out from the neighbouring farm.

The production of rabbit meat presented little difficulty, for although there were dandelions, soft thistles, dock leaves and other species of herbage available most of the year, the animals actually became by-products of our vegetable stall, thriving on carrot tops, bruised apples and the outer leaves of cabbages and cauliflowers but with clean hay and rolled oats always available.

When their litters were due the does would make a cosy nest in the hay and line it with soft fur that they had pulled away from beneath their bodies. For seven days or so they must not be disturbed, for the offspring are blind and bald and any handling can easily make the mother forsake her babies, but in due course it was always delightful to see the little miniatures when they began to scamper round the cage.

One day the fine big buck that had been flown across from England for breeding purposes began to hold his head on one side and I could see no possible reason whatsoever why he should do so. I thought he enjoyed his life and hadn't a care in the world, but his plight got worse and he began to lose weight and couldn't stand up properly. After making enquiries I eventually established that the poor fellow had lost his sense of balance, an ailment that is considered incurable and if appropriate action had not been taken he would surely have starved to death.

A young replacement had to be imported, was duly introduced to the six mature unrelated females and production continued.

A rabbit has a double digestive system scientifically called coprophagy which involves quite an amazing procedure, for he only has one simple stomach and can't juggle around his partly digested fibres from one depot to another, like the goats do. Instead, he passes currents that are some hard, some soft, they may even be sweet and sour, I don't know, but the soft ones he certainly pops back in his mouth while they're still warm!

Some of the nutrients absorbed from this redigestion of soft droppings are absolutely essential to his health. So, if you happen to notice your tame Bunny carrying out some unusual contortions in the corner of his hutch, please don't disturb, he might be just enjoying his "business lunch".

CHAPTER 32

IN THE SMOKE

DURING the fishing season hundreds of barrels become lined up along the Island's quaysides each one filled to the brim with freshly landed herrings and shovels-full of salt, all ready for shipment to Holland, Germany, Poland and even further afield.

Many generations of Manx folk have known the herring to play a very important part in their survival. The crofters would scratch an existence from their piece of land but would very much need to set sail and gain a share of the harvest from the sea as well, every household used to have its crock of salties and many still do today.

One of the simplest and yet most satisfying dishes ever to be served to a person coming home from a day of heavy-going outdoor activities requires just a couple of herrings, a few large potatoes and a raw onion. This is the traditional "spuds an' herring" that has brought so many hungry families through hard times in the past.

Fay's particular method of preparation was slightly varied by a Scottish influence for she was certainly no stranger to the "silver darlings". Fresh herrings were by far the best but when salties were used they generally needed soaking in cold water overnight, but the actual length of time depended upon just how long they had been preserved, whether it be days, weeks or even months. The potatoes were scrubbed but not peeled, boiled in a large pan until found tender to the prongs of a fork, then all the water poured away, the fish laid on top of the piping hot spuds (still in the pan) and simply covered with a cloth, left to stand for five minutes and then served onto a plate with a couple of slices of raw onion.

Absolutely delicious, I could really relish a couple at this very moment, though I've only been sitting on my back-side at a typewriter all morning.

Unfortunately this so basic but so very nutritional meal still carries its association with poverty and is falling into less frequent, use, but times can change, especially if foreign powers continue to scoop out of the sea thousands of tons of living creatures, all destined to be ground down for the production of fertiliser, this must surely be rocking the ecological boat.

Doesn't it seem ironic that if you pick up a book on household management of only a hundred years ago, you can read guidance for the general hiring and firing of labour and learn that it was regarded as reasonable for the servants to be provided with food but to be given the understanding that they would not be expected to accept salmon on more than two occasions each week.

In the north of the Island the wartime hangars of a disused airport had been put to light industrial use, but amongst them could be found a couple of smaller buildings devoted to the collection and resale of assorted secondhand junk which I frequently found worthy of a few minutes perusal. Several items had turned up at these depots for which I could identify an immediate and important use. One such object was a canning machine, not too large, it could take just one can at a time and could easily be clamped onto our kitchen table, just what we wanted.

Unfortunately none of the blank empty cans could be found anywhere on the Island and it took at least a dozen phone calls across the water to establish where they were still being manufactured in that size and to arrange transportation.

Our initial enthusiasm to use the newly acquired plaything gave instant visions of the forthcoming programme to be, "eat what you can and can what you can't". Culminating in the pantry shelves displaying fifty-seven varieties of home production.

Fourteen tough old-timers were brought home from a poultry mart for very little money, pressure cooked, skilfully seasoned and canned. A big success, they tasted just like chicken but we kept opening another can for the sheer delight of showing each other just how smart we were.

Next we arranged to collect a quantity of large dog fish from friends who went out fishing and would normally have thrown them overboard as undesirable anyhow. I quite enjoyed the flavour of their large steaks of white fish meat with its absence of bone, except for one long flexible piece leading from head to tail. The only inconvenience being the necessary skinning which was just like heaving away at sheets of tough, wet, coarse, black sandpaper. We'd had to consult reference books to establish all this canning procedure and were a little set-back when reading that fish must be boiled and boiled in the cans for at least five hours for fear of bacteria and the dreaded botulism.

The interest began to wane slightly for, although the contents were costing us so little, there had been the expenditure of the cans plus their carriage across the water, and to keep a large container on the boil for hour after hour took an awful lot of timber. We were already thriving on an intake of so many fresh, wholesome ingredients so why should we suddenly change our entire eating policy and start eating tinned stuff, just because I found a cheap machine in a junk shop?

Kippers had become a family favourite every so often, for on the Island they are smoked in the old fashioned way, hung in kilns from tenterhooks, not just painted with an edible varnish. The easiest preparation for the table is just to pop them in a tall jug, fill it with boiling water and in two or three minutes your kipper is ready to fall off the bone, without sending that savoury stench all round the house you get from a kippery frying pan.

Inevitably there was bound to come a time when the Heath Robinson-like urge to make my own smoking unit would become irresistible, with thoughts of smoked salmon, smoked pork, smoked leg of lamb very much in the fore.

The prospect of using one of the pigsties did not merit much serious consideration, for I wasn't going to crawl in and out through a hole in the wall to add more fuel or to establish that my potential savouries were not turning to chunks of burnt toast; no, it would have to be a free-standing contraption designed so the fire could be stoked from below, with a removable lid on top to periodically check what was going on inside.

There were a couple of dustbin-style failures that either blew out or just did not get enough air to stay in and then, in the course of one of my routine inspections of other people's throw-outs at the airport junk shop I spotted the ideal piece of equipment.

Some years ago a type of clothes drier was on the market which consisted of an oblong shaped metal box, that stood on end, with an electric heating element in the base and a removable lid at the top which revealed a row of narrow wooden slats from which could be suspended a dozen or so babies nappies. Just what I needed.

Arriving home with my exciting purchase there was of course a beloved wife to greet me with the usual critical salutation she reserves for whenever I launch myself into the creation of a scientific project. "Oh no! Not more rubbish."

Nevertheless, with a few modifications it was soon ready for testing, for I'd removed the electrical fittings from down below, leaving the base now completely open and having experimented with a large tin can punched full of holes and filled with a blend of hardwood chippings and sawdust, knew that a good volume of suitable smoke could definitely be produced.

The procedure was to get the smoke producer ignited with methylated spirits (not paraffin because of the flavour) then as soon as the fuel was smouldering well and pouring out dense smoke, the clothes drier could be lifted up bodily and placed directly over the top.

The first unfortunates to be condemned for sacrifice were three dozen fresh mackerel, they were suspended from separate hooks cut from wire coat hangers and after about an hour we took one out and it was almost perfect, the remainder were given extra time but unfortunately when the lid was lifted once again several of them had become so tenderly cooked that they'd dropped off their hooks into the smouldering ash below. There were still improvements to be made but I gained an unanimous decision that the junk shop smoker was a success, and that was quite something!

CHAPTER 33

TRADER'S TALES

EACH winter was our period of relaxation for, apart from the Friday and Saturday trading days, the time could be spent on carrying out more and more home improvements and generally pottering around amongst the livestock. Spring however brought busy preparation for the holiday season, the market had to be thoroughly cleaned out, smartened up with a pot of paint here and there, cartons of merchandise were to be opened and checked against any pilferage in transit and then the contents individually priced, ready for the hectic few weeks ahead when we needed to have the money flowing through the till.

Normally throughout the summer I would rise between four and five each morning and attend to all clerical work, sales graphs, correspondence and so on, washing away any complications with my favourite pint pot full of tea and with a soft background of foreign radio programmes.

Seven o'clock was the time to disturb Fay with tea and toast before going out to milk the goats and attend to the chicks, ducks, rabbits and pigs in the calm cool freshness of the morning before setting off for a day of shopkeeping.

Between home and the Quayside Market there were six producers with whom I had an arrangement to pick up sprouts, cabbages, cauliflowers, turnips, tomatoes, cucumbers, etc., according to what was available at the time of the year, with barely deviating from the main route. Consequently little time was lost but I was able to offer farm produce that had been freshly picked or cut that very morning.

Magnificent prize-winning onions could always be seen at the various horticultural shows that took place on the Island but I never managed to find a person who was growing them on a commercial scale, so it was necessary to make my purchases through the Douglas dealer who had a buyer standing on the Liverpool wholesale market. Each time a net of onions was delivered I was always interested to read the country of origin, one thinks of Spain as being the most obvious source but it was quite surprising to find that shipments were also coming from America and even as far afield as New Zealand. The freight and handling charges must have formed quite a large percentage of the price involved.

When the fruit and vegetables had all been unloaded, placed on display and with Tony safely deposited in school, his mother and I were ready to face the public.

The green grocery section had been promulgated initially as a means whereby the shopper could be enticed inside the building to buy perhaps a lettuce which bore only a few coppers profit but we really hoped that some more expensive, more lucrative, item of clothing would be spotted and maybe purchased at a later visit. Quite quickly however, the greenery business developed and began to need my full-time attendance. The attractiveness of the display was very important, apples could be polished up and snow-white cauliflowers evenly trimmed and neatly stacked, but the customer would always know exactly which one she wanted and it would invariably be that which was the cornerstone of my artistic display.

Customers became identifiable by their own particular requirements, one lady with small children would always want small bananas, another required large firm specimens for use in fruit salad, whereas another, whom I recognised whenever she entered the building, would ask if I'd kept her any black spotted ones. Certainly a little over-ripeness does improve the flavour considerably.

Mushrooms had to be firm and curled underneath for, if they were fully opened they were expected to be cheaper. Tomatoes had to be of uniform size and not too large and sometimes I was asked whether they had tough skins. Brussel sprouts had to be like hard tight little balls of leaves for if I bought any that were loosely open, like flowers, no person whatsoever would take them.

Strawberries and raspberries could only be purchased in small quantities for if unsold they would be covered with grey furry mould the following morning, of interest only to the goats, which would seem such sacrilege even at the growers' price.

The situation was ideal for people wishing to pull up right outside the door and have a bag of potatoes dumped straight into the boot of their car. I learnt to identify and appreciate that there were different flavours with the various varieties of potatoes and I had to be prepared to correctly answer such questions as, would they be disappointingly soft and soggy when boiled? Would they be light and fluffy when mashed? Would they make good chips?

Sometimes they would ask if I could carry out delivery. "Certainly, no bother at all", I used to say. But one day I was given an address that seemed within walking distance rather than bringing the van from where it was parked. I strode along with the spuds on my shoulder and then found that the address was a flat at the top of four flights of stairs.

All good exercise I suppose, but every so often I had to go for a session with an osteopath to get a bit of flexibility eased back into my spine.

We met a fascinating cross-section of the community and every day seemed to have its entertaining highlight. One day a fisherman walked into the building, he looked around at the rails and shelves all loaded with clothing and then came straight up to me, as I stood behind the vegetable counter, and with a soft brogue he asked, "Do you sell men's ties Master?"

That was one bargain line that we didn't stock but I detected a certain pathetic urgency in the situation. Sure enough, the fellow was due to appear in Court in five minutes time, so I whipped off my own tie and handed it across.

Away he went, and I've no idea what his trouble had been or what was the outcome, but I do know that later in the day my tie was returned, neatly folded and with it was a big bag of Dublin Bay prawns that must have been worth about four new ties.

There were packages to collect, parcels to deliver and Tony to be brought from school, then, when all the shoppers had gone home there was the clearing up to be done, dust sheets put in position over all the stock, cabbage leaves and other garbage to be swept up and loaded into the van then, at least, we were rolling along again towards Ballaneddin.

While Fay busied herself in the kitchen, for we didn't normally manage to get a meal at mid-day, I cleared out the van and fed its contents to the animals. The goats had their second milking and the eggs were collected and only then could I come indoors, have a good wash, settle down to some very welcome meal, usually with a glass of something or other alongside, before watching the nine-o'clock news then away to bed. To awake at dawn again the next morning, fully refreshed and looking forward to the day ahead.

People might have got the impression that most of the vegetables sold in our market had been grown by ourselves, but this was far from true, there were just not enough hours in a day to do everything we would like to.

Certainly we had our own tomatoes in the greenhouse and lettuce we used were often taken straight from the garden but beyond that, more or less all of our stock-in-trade was produced by commercial growers. The exception to the case was the artichoke, for this was certainly a home product, not the Globe artichoke with its edible flower-head, no, the other one, the Jerusalem, with its potato-like tubers. They will grow very well in almost any district, but if the soil is reasonable and a bit sandy they will grow larger and not so knobbly.

If dug from the garden and cooked straight away one gains the maximum flavour, but this produces an unfortunate side-effect in the form of a remarkable amount of wind within all who have participated. Fortunately we found that if the tasty vegetable was kept for at least a day after harvesting, before being boiled, then the problem no longer applied.

Thank goodness too, for life at Ballaneddin was bad enough already, with an impolite bulldog in the household.

CHAPTER 34

AT WORK AND PLAY

RETAILERS, as with any other business, must methodically record their sales, cost of sales, gross profit, expenses and overheads. Not only for their own advantage but also in a manner that is acceptable to the Inland Revenue people and be prepared to pay taxation on any subsequent profits gained. No-one enjoys handing over a portion of their income to the Government but even the most begrudging tax payer realises that the collection of a revenue from some source or other is essential to the running of the country.

Announcements began to appear in the press of an entirely new form of taxation, not an Income Tax, not a Purchase Tax, but something absolutely different which was to be known as Value Added Tax. Apparently each time an item changed hands in an improved form or increased price there was to be a percentage added for Westminster to spend.

I greeted these official proclamations with the same complete lack of enthusiasm as did thousands of other small business people, maybe even less, for there must surely have been the possibility that it wouldn't be accepted over here. Particularly as we were only just becoming accustomed to use of the decimalisation system. *(People said it would never catch on in the north of the Island.)*

Even when the local papers broke the news that Manx legislation had been passed to incorporate V.A.T. I still bore that forlorn optimism of a "*perhaps it will go away*" attitude. Only when large envelopes marked O.H.M.S. began tumbling through the letter box did I take the matter seriously and begin wading through the literature.

First of all I doubted my own interpretation of the rules of this new taxation game, it seemed so ridiculcous and couldn't possibly be true. The wording of the publications, more and more kept arriving, was not too complicated provided you had the time to spare and possessed the patience required to go through page after page, word by word, to gain an understanding.

My own particular conclusion, after a certain amount of head scratching and bewilderment, was that if I were to hold the most humble item in the store, say a simple coat hanger, in my hand I could see that it was an assembly of one curved piece of wood, through which had been poked a metal hook then finished off with a lick of paint or varnish.

That finished item had however, at one time been a small piece of living tree, a shovel-full of iron ore and a minute portion of whatever ingredients are used at a paint factory. So, as separate units they may have passed through a forestry depot, a saw mill, timber merchant, iron foundry, wire-works, chemical factory and so on before being assembled as a coat hanger. In each instance value had been added and therefore taxation charged. The manufacturer might sell to a wholesaler having added further tax, the wholesaler would then sell to a concern supplying shop-fittings at a profit plus further tax and the next time I needed a gross of coat hangers there would be tax to pay upon the overall figure.

That seemed to be the bad news, but, by reading further through the selection of booklets so freely provided, there seemed to be happier times ahead for, I could send in a claim to the V.A.T. Office and they would refund *all* the tax I'd paid on those coat hangers. The shop fitter could also claim back what tax he'd been charged by the wholesaler; the wholesaler could regain the tax he'd paid to the manufacturer who in turn would reclaim all that had been added to his wood, wire and paint. So the whole incredible operation seemed to go all the way back to the fellows with the axes and the shovels, rendering a minute amount of revenue for a mammoth quantity of paper work involving calculated additions to every invoice, all to be checked, cross checked and balanced, on a monetary merry-go-round.

A wide range of goods was available in our Quayside Market, mostly subject to tax but not necessarily at the same precise percentage and any customer could quite freely select items from varying categories and bring them along to the till for payment in one transaction. Itemising these separate commodities did not present much difficulty but when I learned that a record was required for every transaction involving variation of tax payable whether it be a reduction by virtue of staff discount, reduction for a soiled garment or a missing button and the inevitable exchanges where a customer comes back the following day requiring an item from a different part of our little store entirely, this all added up to much more paper-work.

When the customer paid his V.A.T. and walked out of the shop he had no means of claiming a tax refund, but at least he did not have to keep endless records and fill up endless forms. The Customs and Excise Office was generally helpful when problems arose, but as I was already working long hours throughout the summer and then had all this additional clerical work thrust upon me, I think perhaps I should have phoned them up and asked "Who the hell's going to milk the goats?"

Although the busy season was comparatively short, the days sometimes seemed very long, standing for hour after hour on the concrete floor and especially if the bell of the till was not ringing very often, life became a bit tedious. One frustrating day when everybody seemed to ask for things we didn't stock but just made their way around the building picking up neatly folded garments from the wooden trays and dropping them back again in an untidy heap, a lady stopped in front of a section bearing a conspicuous sign reading "SCHOOL SKIRTS" and holding a green one above her head she shouted across the building to Fay, "Is this one of the green school skirts?" "No!" came the reply, "It's a jar of pickled cabbage".

Fortunately both women then burst out laughing and the till duly chimed out approvingly.

Another day however when I was in the refreshment area a young man stuck his head through the take-away hatch and shouted, "What have you got in ice lollies?" "Sticks", I replied, but he just walked away shaking his head from side to side and never came back.

In the working day conversations on the Quayside I was generally completely outnumbered by chattering womenfolk, one can certainly have too much of a good thing, but, by a stroke of sheer good fortune rather than any involvement of management, it so happened that the premises destined to become the Quayside Market had been built almost back to back with a public house. So, provided everything was well under control and Fay had appropriate staff alongside, I was able to slip out of the building and just a few strides would take me through a nearby agricultural depot and into the public bar by means of the back door.

With an almost all male clientele and with good beer and good conversation readily available, without the distraction of either juke box or pool table, it offered me those little breaks from business that I so needed.

A television set was perched up on a shelf in one corner of the room but this was reserved for viewing sporting activities only. Other programmes would surely have been detrimental to the general atmosphere. Apart from the Island's own fixtures there was great interest in events across the water, particularly association football, and on one particularly memorable occasion a well known local character who was an ardent supporter of Liverpool F.C. became subjected to quite a lot of good humoured criticism about the ability of his favourite players.

The conversation concentrated upon the anticipated outcome of a match at the forthcoming weekend. The big, good-humoured fellow said all he could to emphasise his confidence, to him defeat seemed an utter impossibility. "If Liverpool were to lose on Saturday I'd crawl along the road in shame", he rather rashly announced.

Part way through the next Saturday afternoon I just nipped out of the Market for a brief fifteen minute breather when the half-time scores flashed onto the screen, Liverpool were one goal down!

Back again in the market I sold a few more vegetables, chatted politely to a couple of old ladies, then hurried out again, past the sacks of grain, and in once more through the back door of the licensed premises. The bar seemed packed, fellows had walked along from other public houses, everyone was watching the final scores as they appeared on the screen.

Suddenly there was a great cheer, Liverpool had been BEATEN!

Without the slightest hesitation the team's disillusioned Manx supporter dropped to the floor, the entire audience then trooped out into the street, some with glasses still in their hands, and brought the traffic to a standstill, till one lone figure crawled through the doorway and made his way on hands and knees right across the roadway then slowly turned and came back again.

Everyone absolutely roared with laughter, never had I seen anything so funny in all my life, the episode had been so spontaneous and absolutely hilarious. Back inside the bar room Liverpool's large, very red faced, very worthy supporter rose again to his feet, joining in the merriment that had been brought about at his own expense. A true sportsman indeed!

Joviality within the Public Houses has for long been very much an accepted part of the Manxman's way of life and, were the facts more widely known, the Island could easily become a veritable

Mecca for all those connoisseurs in Britain who spend much of their spare time in pursuit of "Real Ale".

An ancient law of the Manx Parliament still absolutely prohibits the slightest form of substitution, concerning the use of malt, hops, sugar and barley, as the basic natural ingredients for brewing ale upon the Isle of Man.

This "Ye Olde Consumer's Protection Act" ensures that none of the quick-brew chemical short-cuts, the use of potato flour and such like, must be incorporated.

I once found it fascinating to see how local brewers carried out their longstanding tradition, even using strange words of their trade from a byegone era and ensuring that after about fourteen days of care and expertise, a veritable nectar is available that any 'Real Ale' man may raise in his hand to wish his fellow men health and happiness.

CHAPTER 35

BREAKAWAY

FAY and I had been so busily involved in the activities of Ballaneddin and the Ramsey harbourside that eight precious years of our lifetime had quickly passed by, and our little baby was now a rapidly growing schoolboy who had only known one family holiday and whose parents both spent every day of the summertime working in the shop.

Our original intention had been to establish a quiet, health-conscious, rural life-style with the aid of a simple part-time trading occupation. Unfortunately however, the business matters were now playing far too great a part in family affairs.

We had endeavoured to build up a reasonable selection of stock in the Market that covered clothing for all ages and purposes but inflation had begun to gallop across the British Isles. Within a short space of time the sums of cash we could designate to each stall and offer the public a selection of say, babyclothes, or perhaps workmens overalls, would now only buy about half the number of garments, so all available funds had to be turned back into the purchase of stock otherwise the premises would soon have looked rather bare.

During the first four years the results had been very satisfactory but latterly we were definitely losing ground, other stores were now seling merchandise within our price range, and double yellow no-parking lines on both sides of our frontage began a gradual strangulation.

Lots of small businesses in England were failing, this certainly seemed to be the wrong era for any independent minded individual to make a livelihood in self-employment. Some visitors from across the water would enjoy the Ballaneddin hospitality, marvel at our good fortune to be living there, but, taking their own holidays-with-pay, pension schemes and sickness payments all very much for granted, and yet wailing about the amount of income tax they paid.

We were heading for a spot of trouble and it was up to me to think of some feasible way out. Already the stage had been reached of worrying each night and instead of waking up in the morning fresh and eager to enjoy every minute of the new day I was turning over facts and figures again and again, knowing that no amount of fresh air, good cooking or herbal tonics could possibly drive away the immediate anxieties.

An involvement whereby quantities of stock were bought on credit, that had to be sold and paid for within a very limited time, was certainly not the life we really wanted, we were both working on a treadmill and did not know how on earth to get off it. Certainly we had a beautiful and by now quite valuable estate in the country, but all this overhanging frustration was taking away our enjoyment. In more normal circumstances people could work hard to establish a small business with the confidence that at some future date it could be disposed of satisfactorily as a going concern, but, for us, this prospect was slowly slipping away.

Then, a little-used word popped out of the dictionary and was suddenly heard upon every pair of lips throughout the Island . . . "MILLENNIUM" . . . for the following year the Isle of Man was to celebrate not a precise anniversary, but at least a thousand years of government by its own parliament of Tynwald.

The Island has never been part of the United Kingdom, Tynwald was established in Viking times in a Scandinavian tradition and although it has been answerable to a variety of English and Scottish Lords of Mann over the centuries, it has maintained right up to the present day a unique degree of self-governing power. Tynwald is responsible for all legislation on the Island's internal affairs including, of course, the setting of its own direct taxation rate. That alone was surely worthy of a great historic pageant.

There was to be dancing in the streets, flags flying everywhere and boatloads of ex-patriots sailing in from all corners of the world. It is said there are a larger number of people, pleased to express their Manx descendance, in the U.S.A. than the entire present-day population of the Island.

The Queen of England, the King of Norway and a host of other dignitaries were scheduled to be in attendance for these unique festivities. They weren't likely to wander into our Market, but nevertheless the overall greatness of the occasion could possibly produce the most profitable year our business had ever known.

What a happy thought! Deeper reflection however brought wonder of what sort of tourism season was likely to follow in the years that would come after the much acclaimed Millennium?

A decision to enter wholeheartedly into any aspect of commercial life has to be made at precisely the right time but it is equally important to know when to get out again without having the fingers burnt. Should we order vast quantities of Millennium souvenirs and then sell off the premises as an empty warehouse a year later? Should we see if a buyer could be found right now, on the eve of this fantastic once-ever opportunity? Now at last there was a definite choice available and a constructive decision to be made rather than suffering any more of that vague uncertainty and getting nowhere.

The choice was certainly made, and indeed in a most decisive and almost spontaneous manner but remarkably influenced by a totally unforeseen happening over in the North of England, where, a frail little widowed lady, living all alone, had answered a knock on her front door.

The man standing on the step was a complete stranger but having established her identity he proceeded to tell her that he had come from London to say that she was due to receive a sum of money from the estate of a long deceased and very distant relative. This was wonderful news and so utterly unexpected but then the bearer of the good tidings produced a document for her to sign, giving him one third of her inheritance, plus legal costs and other expenses, before he would reveal any further details. The kind hearted soul who had opened that door was someone I remembered so well from earliest days, she was a surviving sister of my own dear mother. Without making comment on the ethics of this bounty hunter and the fee involved I'll simply add that in due course I too received a cheque for a small portion of the same estate.

Hurrah! It was just like winning on the football pools, when you haven't even posted a coupon!

The sum involved could have been very easily paid into the business, as the introduction of further capital, but it would have been just a clerical entry, significant only by an extra few dozen pairs of jeans it might have introduced into stock.

"This is such a lovely windfall, let's do something very special with it . . . let's buy some new carpet for the hall and stairway!" said Fay, always so quick off the mark with a domestic possibility.

Fortunately, she found my own proposition far more exciting, for I suggested we should close the shop at the end of the season, hand over the keys to our friend the estate agent, tell him to sell, then buzz off the Island for a month.

Once I'd parried all the thrusts of "What about the goats? What about the chickens? What about the rabbits? and most important, what about Tony's school?" she was very excited. "Where are we going?" came the next and most obvious question.

"We'll load up the car and this cheque is enough to take us across the Irish sea to Liverpool, across the North Sea to Holland, and to fill the tank with petrol several times, so I'll drive you round Europe."

CHAPTER 36

NEVER AGAIN

NOT long after reaching our decision to take a complete break, and all the complicated arrangements had been carried out to ensure the well-being of the livestock during our absence; when even the goldfish had been found a temporary home, we at last drove along in the morning sunshine to take our previously booked position aboard the vessel that would transport the three of us with our fully loaded car on the initial stage of our get-away holiday.

The mooring ropes were released and we eased gently away from the harbour wall to carve a passage through the clear blue Manx water, heading eastwards for England, as we watched our little paradise Island settle down into the horizon farther and farther astern.

Ahead was to be the excitement and nostalgia of meeting relatives and friends in places that my wife and I had once known so well, but for our young schoolboy son it was to be an educational adventure away from the shelter of his more law-abiding environment and it was a rather sad reflection upon present-day society when his first instructions were to be that from now onwards the car must always be locked when left unattended and that any any stranger attempting to make conversation with him must be regarded with caution.

In the early afternoon we churned our way through the murky, polluted water of the Mersey estuary, then disembarked into that density of traffic at Liverpool's Pier Head we had left behind a few years earlier. Both our elder boys were now young married men and our first overnight stay was across country to the outskirts of York, where Roger, having gained engineering experience on the

Continent and in Africa, had now returned to England and set up home with his wife and two children.

There had been so much to talk about, for the one draw-back to our self-imposed island life was the limited time that could be spent with our children and grandchildren. We were certainly very delighted to find the young family so happily settled into their newly acquired home in a picturesque village.

Our next move was towards Hull, where we boarded another, somewhat larger vessel that this time was to take us overnight to Holland. Included within the sailing ticket was not only a very comfortably furnished cabin but also the provision of a splendid evening meal whereby an excellent selection of both English and Continental dishes were made available on an eat-as-much-as-you-like basis.

Fully refreshed and breakfasted we then rolled off onto the Rotterdam dockside and motored away from the industrial installations into the flat, very productive, agricultural scenery for which the country is so renowned.

Some large, traditional windmills were still standing while others of smaller and of less conventional design were busily pumping water and generating electricity. No land seemed to be wasted and everywhere was so clean and tidy. As we drove along that morning it was quite remarkable to see how many ladies were outside their homes polishing the windows. Wherever we stopped the people were very friendly and helpful, most of whom seemed to have learned English as a second language.

Driving right across Holland we then crossed through the frontier. post into Germany and although now into the month of October the weather was so particularly favourable we had been able to picnic on a variety of local sausage-meats in warm sunshine at the side of the Black Forest.

Out of Germany we passed into Belgium where we stopped and watched men playing roadside games with solid metal bowls, before continuing south into Luxemburg. The crossing of some of these international frontiers has become such a mere formality these days that when using the minor roads, as we did, close to an invisible meandering demarcation line it is quite possible that a few miles of mother's faulty navigation could bring about the ridiculous question, 'Well, what country are we in now, Daddy?'

When at home, Tony and his little pals spent many happy hours playing at soldiers but as we left Luxemburg and entered France I deliberately headed towards the historic town of Verdun, believing that by now my son was becoming old enough to be given a grim insight into what soldiering had really been like. It was here that to a rallying call of 'They shall not pass' thousands upon thousands of young men had rushed forward against enemy machine guns, to be mercilessly scythed down or blown to pieces in the shell holes they reached.

At the military cemetery we wandered slowly along, in quiet respect, between the rows and rows of simple white crosses. The air was quite still and we tiptoed across the pathways to reduce the crunch of gravel. Each cross bore a young man's name and age; all killed years before we were even born but there was the harrowing thought of what the future might have in store. I took Fay's hand for she too was reading the crosses, but thinking Roger – Malcolm – Roger – Malcolm: they'd all been some mother's sons.

We walked inside the huge white sepulchre where every stone bore a name in remembrance and we peered through the glass panels at the base of the building at the mass of skulls and other human debris that lay amongst the foundations, for this building was a tribute to over one hundred thousand soldiers whose poor bodies had been torn apart beyond all identification.

Along part of this battle site near the end of hostilities the order had been given to "Fix bayonets" but the men in one particular trench were still awaiting the command to "Charge" for heavy shellfire had buried them all alive. A line of rusty bayonets still protrude above the surface of the rubble held by skeletons in a standing grave.

From Verdun we drove further south towards Bar-le-duc some thirty miles away, along the only highway in the country that does not bear an official number, for this is France' "SACRED ROAD". Along which every kilometer stone is topped by a soldier's helmet and where one can walk along for mile after mile of its length, knowing that for every stride you take one hundred men had been slaughtered along that section of the Western Front.

We paused from time to time and I answered all Tony's questions to the best of my ability, trying to visualise the tragic scenes of earlier in the century when that part of France's countryside lay in utter desolation, churned over time and again with heavy artillery. I spoke of the trenches, the wounded horses, the barbed wire, the mud and the blood, in an effort to deglamourise his thoughts of warfare, but remembering quite well that at his age I could go to the shoe cupboard and take out with pride and excitement the pair of "Puttees", lengths of khaki coloured woollen material, and wrap them round the calves of my legs as my father had done in his army days.

This had been a very solemn few hours of our holiday and, although I was driving, my thoughts were very much of those days gone by when infantrymen had marched along towards the front line singing "Pack up your troubles" getting nearer and nearer to the stench of the dead compatriots they were soon to join. My over-all feelings were that *this must never, never happen again*, almost as if I was a guide, fully conversant with the horrors of trench warfare, who was taking a couple of younger companions on a conducted tour.

Surely it must have been the wine and the cognac I had taken at lunchtime, coupled with general motoring fatigue, for I had certainly lapsed for a short while into a state of absent mindedness. It wasn't until I saw a signpost pointing to the left, bearing the name of a village I knew very well, that my thoughts were jolted back abruptly to the stark awareness that another wretched European Bloodbath *HAD ALREADY TAKEN PLACE!*

More mechanised and highly technical than ever before, when suicidal bayonet charges had been partially replaced by little teams of men huddled inside bombing aircraft who flew time and again deep into enemy territory to cause death and destruction right inside the heart of the nation, each man knowing that four percent of those attacking aircraft would "fail to return". A gamble with life that he'd have to take again and again for thirty times to complete his operational tour, before Squadron survivors, if any, qualified for a rest from activities.

I myself had been within the age group deemed mature enough for slaughter. Twenty-five years after the last young infantryman had been butchered on the barbed wire, I had parachuted down in moonlight alongside that SACRED ROAD, while my bomber blazed and exploded where it had crashed, near the village that was signposted.

IT MUST NEVER HAPPEN AGAIN, AGAIN!

Several times since the war I have made my nostalgic pilgrimage to that region of France, where I have always been greeted as a returning member of the family by the various households who recall my year of false identity and clandestine activities.

That tragic international bloodletting had brought out the worst in some and the best in others.

From those days of fear and hunger I will never forget my indebtedness to, and admiration of, those everyday people who became the French Resistance Movement.

CHAPTER 37

HOME AGAIN

THE entire family tour had been carried out absolutely on schedule. We'd returned to England by crossing the Channel during half an hour of noisy vibration aboard a hovercraft and then, just one month after leaving home, we drove once more up the ramp onto the Douglas bound I.O.M. steamer at Liverpool.

We'd motored over two thousand miles, into six different countries, talked well into the night with so many friends, but now, the three of us were quite thankful of a few hours complete relaxation during the homeward voyage. The holiday had been mentally stimulating but at the same time quite physically exhausting, Fay and I had needed a complete break from our routine and we'd certainly had onè, Tony had missed one month's schooling but had now gained the experience of having an educational peep of life beyond the coastline of his island.

Leaving the main road, passing between the two stone pillars and down the holly-lined driveway, we saw again our Ballaneddin, standing magnificently amongst the tints of the huge sycamores and chestnuts in their autumn glory, a setting that we appreciated even more than ever. . . . There's definitely no place like home!

Reunions were made with our livestock and we quickly caught up with the general news of happenings upon the Island but the information that was to have the most far reaching effect upon our entire future was that during our absence a gentleman had expressed a wish to purchase our Quayside Market premises, for an entirely different use.

A satisfactory agreement was reached, contracts exchanged and a great closing down sale was proclaimed in which there were to be FANTASTIC REDUCTIONS! EVERYTHING MUST GO!!! (and it did).

The disposal of the stock presented very little difficulty for although the initial purchasing had been very much on a trial and error basis there had been very few mistakes and no build-up whatsoever of non-selling items. At one stage we had imported goods directly to the Island from the Far East but found the procedure too involved and time consuming for our size of establishment. (It was straightforward to buy via the importers and manufacturers in England.)

But one amusing incident had taken place concerning a consignment of gents brightly coloured check shirts, they were red and black, green and black and yellow with black, spread over a complete range of sizes, many dozens of garments involved. I was busy opening up the cartons on the very night when we had already arranged to attend a social evening which was to take the form of a "Barn Dance and Cowboy Supper".

"This is just what you need", said Fay, picking out a gaudy red and black shirt in my size.

A few hours later, round about midnight, I was wearing my brand new shirt, a pair of denim jeans and had a toy six-shooter stuck in my belt. The pace had been hot, the drums and guitars had been hammering out some form of rhythm in the subdued lighting while everyone did a jive, a shuffle, or a hokey-cokey to their hearts content in an atmosphere of smoke, beer, hot-dogs, hamburgers and perspiration.

"What on earth has happened to you?" demanded my beloved, when we chanced to meet, travelling in opposite directions under the better illumination of the passageway leading to the toilets. No wonder she'd been surprised, for the black dye was rubbing out of my shirt onto my neck, my hands, and with all the times I'd wiped my forehead and pushed my hair out of my eyes in the course of a very energetic evening, was all over my face.

Next weekend a big pile of shirts stood in a corner of the Quayside market alongside an almost full-size cartoon of a quick-on-the-draw sheriff firing away and at the same time saying "Get your GUN SMOKE shirts here folks!" We sold them all off at a very reasonable price, telling every potential ranch-hand to throw them in the washing machine before wearing, and for years to come Fay and I were to see satisfied customers around the Island still wearing that special bargain line of Gun Smoke Shirts.

Many of our regular customers knew we'd spent a month abroad travelling as far as Germany and some even thought we had brought a lot of brand new stock back with us, perhaps the

Teutonic sounding notice I'd pinned up over a particularly good line in ladies brassieres was causing some confusion . . . "DIESEL STOPPUMFLOPPIN".

I would certainly miss the humorous moments of the market style shop-keeping but the property had so greatly appreciated in value during our ownership that this single transaction turned over an entire page in our lives. At last we were to be free of all anxiety over mortgage repayments and bank commitments. We owned a lovely home, with land. We had our toy-town farmstock plus some capital invested, the income from which could be easily augmented by taking in paying guests for "Farmhouse Holidays" during the summer.

We were absolutely delighted, we danced and hugged each other, "Yippee, we've cracked it!" was the household catch-phrase that could be heard even as we sat up in bed each morning. We hadn't gained a fortune, but all we'd ever wanted was health and peace of mind, the ups and downs of the romantic pantomime were over, from now onwards the principal characters were to play the part where the storyteller says "and they both lived happily ever after".

Certain formalities had to be completed following the closure of the business, one of which involved the sending of a very brief letter to sever my past relationship with the V.A.T. Office, which I followed by unceremoniously ramming all their publications into the kitchen stove. There were booklets called V.A.T. News number one, number two, number three, and so on, dozens of them had been delivered through the post, some had not even been opened, but at least I'd kept them, and they gave off quite a good heat.

Some weeks later however, I was surprised to find that I was still under a legal obligation to fill in another return, this time it would read purchases nil, sales nil, tax charged nil, and remittance herewith enclosed (yes, you've guessed) nil.

Not wishing to die in a fit of laughter I picked up the telephone and my call was answered by a pleasant helpful-to-the-end voice with comforting words explaining that, no doubt accountancy and legal services had been involved in the course of my exit from business activity and each such office had spent time calculating how much Value-Added-Tax they were required to charge against me, now however, I could fill in my form and claim every penny back again.

I never did understand that comic money-go-round but it certainly seemed to keep a lot of people employed, and I for one, was not going to let it worry me any more.

CHAPTER 38

LOVE ON THE FARM

THE feelings of satisfaction and relief must surely have shown very clearly on our faces, we were absolutely revelling in the utter joy of our good fortune, from now on we could concentrate entirely upon the country life we loved.

Each morning I woke up early, so completely relaxed and happy, no more worries, every day was to be the first day of the rest of my life and I was going to fully enjoy each minute that came. In a modest way I'd reached retirement while still active enough to enjoy all those things that had been scheduled for "some day", if time ever permitted. I'd had a very lucky life and the best was yet to come.

Twiggy, the old barrel shaped bulldog bitch, who had made so many undignified exits from the farmyard with poultry pecking at her backside and had waited so patiently for our return from business each day, had now died.

The much travelled tail-less cat who had been born on the Island, reared in England, then returned with us later, had formed a unique relationship for several years whereby a British Bulldog and a Manx cat enjoyed a peaceful co-existence within one basket but she too passed quietly away very shortly afterwards. Time keeps going by and it catches everybody eventually.

We learnt that a very alert young black and white border collie puppy was needing a good home, both his parents were hard-working sheepdogs but once he reached Ballaneddin all his intelligence and instinct was confined to such a small scale of farmlife he became just a very obedient, gentle, tolerant, family pet.

One particularly wet and stormy day I happened to notice a slight movement in some hay that was lying in the corner of an outbuilding. There was a tiny kitten, frail, pitifully thin and could not have been inside very long for it was soaking wet. I've no idea where it could have come from but when I took the poor little creature indoors to show Tony and his mother it was very soon recovering in a cosy little box close to the kitchen stove.

Within a few months it had developed into a healthy young female who lived outside but was often seen in the vicinity of the house and could be picked up and would purr appreciatively in response to gentle stroking. In due course she received the amorous attentions of visiting Toms, some from nearby homes, others probably half wild, and subsequently produced an annual quantity of kittens in assorted colouring which were stumpys, rumpys, half-tail and full length pussy cats. (The difference between a stumpy and a rumpy is that one offspring is born with no tail at all, but has just one vertebra protruding, whereas the other has no tail at all, at all.)

They would grow up to be completely self-supporting, taught by their mother to hunt the ample supplies of small birds, mice and baby rabbits in the hedgerows, till old enough to move on and establish their own territory in the countryside. We could always see at least one feline specimen snooping around the rear of the house on the offchance that some tit-bit might be thrown in its direction, or that the kitchen door might accidentally be left ajar. Only a few seconds were needed for a rapid self-service operation to take place, whereby the meat for the family's evening meal could disappear from the kitchen table. Those pretty little furry kittens invariably grew up to become wretched thieving creatures that were utterly untrustworthy.

For only a few second were needed for a rapid self-service operation to take place, whereby the meat for the family's evening meal could disappear from the kitchen table. Those pretty little furry kittens invariably grew up to become wretched thieving creatures that were utterly untrustworthy.

Really, the worst thing we could do was to start putting any form of foodstuff outside the house for a new litter of kittens, for they would all grow up and tell their friends and the situation became so ridiculous at one stage that whenever I stepped outside in the morning to empty the ashes and bring in some more logs, there would be no fewer than seven cats peering down from strategic positions along the wall, on the workshop roof and halfway up the walnut tree, each one poised for the daily battle of wits where one false move could deprive me of my breakfast. I even had to fit wire mesh over the goldfish tank, for Fay had to rescue Moby Dick one day from the clutches of two sets of needle sharp claws. Fortunately the fish survived for several years afterwards and grew quite large on its daily diet of breadcrumbs and its weekly garden worm.

Only one cat ever became reliable enough to attain the recognised status as being the family pet, he was a tortoise-shell coloured Tom whom we named as "Tigger". He never stole anything, he just lazed around and three queens brought along all the rabbits and sparrows he needed.

The rest of the farm stock all seemed quite healthy and contented, in the poultry house a fine looking rooster maintained the discipline where, each evening, a strict positioning on the perches was adhered to in accordance with the pecking order of the feathered society. Some were more privileged than others, but he seemed to spread a little happiness around everyone in general; in any case there was an enthusiastic young bantam cock there also, and he would tackle absolutely anything that stood still long enough.

Old Charlie Drake, the Muscovy duck, was no longer around but his successor, Young Charlie, still favoured his father's choice of venue for romance and ecstasy inside the rainwater bath.

Inside the rabbit house the heavy, meat producing buck now had six specially selected breeding does but he was separately caged and his performances were entirely at my discretion.

We now had three mature nanny goats who would come running down from the paddock twice a day. When I banged my hand on the side of a bucket and called their names they'd go straight inside the old shippen and each in turn jump on to a wooden bench ready to be milked in an upright operation, rather than me having the back-breaking procedure of filling a bucket down on the ground.

Burying my forehead into the animal's belly I would start the

rhythmic left-right-left-right action, going squirt, squirt, squirt into the bottom of the empty bucket which would return a sound of zip-zip-zip-zip until it became muffled by a blanket of warm milky foam into a purr-purr-purr-purr that would have to be maintained for quite a while. It's no use looking expectantly down into the bucket hoping for a gallon of fresh milk to miraculously appear, even if the animal happened to have been endowed with a fine big pair of tits, it still took about a hundred squeezes to extract even the first pint, you must keep up the steady rhythm, never mind the aching wrists, think of something else, you'll eventually get used to it. Wearing wellington boots, old patched and faded jeans and an open neck shirt I inhaled the steamy aroma of the froth, as it mounted inside the bucket and blended with the basic rustic smell of a clean animal's healthy body. Feeling very much part of the creature's way of life, just as they had become so much a part of mine, and I enjoyed it that way, squirt, squirt, squirt, squirt.

When each nanny's bag had been bounced firmly but gently up and down to release the final strippers and the once firm udders hung limply like deflated sausages, away the trio went once more up the paddock, to gain replenishment amongst the assorted vegetation.

An amount was allocated to the ever vigilant row of pussycats, whose faces gazed thirstily down from the hay loft throughout the milking procedure, and the remainder went straight into the house where it was strained through paper tissue and cooled in the refrigerator. Throughout most of the year the flock of three provided the household with over a gallon per day and that was quite ample for the domestic requirments which included of course plenty of home-made cheese and yogurt but a higher yield could have easily been obtained by making dairy nuts and other forms of concentrated foodstuffs available.

The annual mating requirement was greatly simplified by borrowing the services of a neighbouring Billy and bringing him to stay in residence for two or three weeks in company with the nannies.

Any Billy normally smells much stronger in the rutting season and our magnificent looking visitor was no exception, with large curved horns and a shaggy beard he seemed quite a fearsome brute but in all my own experience I've found goats to be quite gentle creatures, even though that big fellow once happened to shake his head abruptly when I was standing alongside and my arm felt as if it had been hit by a rolling pin.

Each year when he was brought along for active duties he would survey the ladies-in-waiting, move to slightly higher ground then, with head raised he would adopt the traditional monarch-of-the-glen stance, a splendid specimen, so photogenic, such an example of rugged beauty.

Then would come the most disgusting ultimate in goathood sex-appeal, he would swing that fine big head down between his front legs and deliberately piddle all over his own face.

Some chaps will do anything for a lady, but that was ridiculous!

CHAPTER 39

A BAD YEAR

THE year of the Isle of Man Millennium got under way with a great fanfare of publicity and our own small classified advertisements produced many enquiries for Farm House Accommodation.

We emptied our wardrobes and moved all personal possessions up into the attic, where we were to spend the summer nights beneath the sloping roof rafters and wondered what sort of people were going to enjoy the privilege of the comfortable bedrooms down below.

The thousand-year-old ceremony was scheduled to take place on the 5th July, and during that week my father and his lifelong pal would be visiting. I was very much looking forward to having the time available to conduct the two old gentlemen around the Island during this period of historic festivity.

Fay's food-store was very well stocked with home-made chutneys, jams, and marmalade. There was ample flour and yeast for breadmaking, one hundredweight sack of sugar and two deep freezes full to capacity with chickens, woodpigeons, rabbits, portions of lamb, hogget, pork and at least a dozen different locally landed forms of sea food. There seemed enough to withstand a twelve months siege, rather than just to satisfy a handful of paying guests.

My father was extremely active for his advanced years and had taken up a later life interest in the production of short newspaper articles and poetry. Hardly a week would pass without his work being published somewhere or other, though frequently under his personal nom-de-plume.

His phone calls were always lighthearted and his letters very

Tynwald Ceremony 1979 — Her Majesty the Queen presiding.

Photograph courtesy of I.O.M. Department of Tourism.

cheerful and uncomplaining, but I had learnt that his physical fitness had begun to deteriorate. Part way through the month of May he rang to see if it would be convenient for himself and his colleague to come over as soon as possible. We were of course, delighted to have them visit us at Ballaneddin as often as they wished, but couldn't just understand what had brought about the apparent urgency, particularly as they were both coming over in July anyway.

When I drove down to the airport, anticipating the friendly wave and beaming smile, I was utterly appalled to recognise the stooped, grey-faced figure who was last to leave the aircraft and move slowly across the tarmac, leaning heavily upon his walking stick and supported by his elderly companion alongside . . . only grim determination was keeping my poor father on his feet.

We reached home safely where he rested awhile, soon looked much better and was able to come down to enjoy his evening meal; but he was still far from the jovial, energetic personality I knew so well. No explanation had been offered for this unscheduled visit but the following day I realised that the grand old fellow knew that his lifespan was almost over, he'd made a stupendous physical effort to reach the Island just once more, and to issue me with his final instructions. He was a remarkable man, his time was running out and he wished to ensure that he left behind his worldly affairs completely in order.

A couple of days later a blue emergency light flashed as the ambulance sped along the country road towards Ballaneddin, answering the doctor's urgently telephoned request. Down the driveway, with the spring foliage brushing its sides, to the front of the house where it semi-circled the central flower garden and reversed towards the front door.

Father had collapsed and for the next few days the doctors fought a losing battle. He lay quietly smiling and softly praising the vigilance and efficiency of the hospital personnel. Then the phone rang ominously early one morning and when the night-sister spoke I knew that never again would I see Pop's friendly smile, but his memory I would cherish and respect for ever.

By now the first of the paying guests had arrived, eager to enjoy a country holiday, their very presence, with the necesssary activities of preparation and presentation of meals helped to ease us over the period of initial shock and they certainly gave very thoughtful consideration to the family distress.

One month after the funeral there was again an early morning phone call, Fay's father had been taken ill overnight and had died in a hospital in England. No more would I see his feats of strength in the farmyard or fathom out his Scottish brogue, Tony had never known his grandmothers and now had lost both Grand-dads in very quick succession.

All the village fêtes and street fairs of the summer and even the magnificent pageant surrounding the world-acclaimed Tynwald ceremony were totally overshadowed by our bereavements and when the visitors had all left the Island and the cool dampness of autumn evenings set in, the peace and tranquility of our homestead took on an atmosphere of empty sadness.

However, there was lots of work to get on with, wood for the stove was to be stock-piled and next year we intended growing additional vegetables, in an area that had been previously fenced off to contain half a dozen pigs while they turned the ground over and over devouring all the roots they unearthed.

By now we had acquired a twenty-year-old tractor that could be started up with petrol but as the carburettor manifold heated up, the fuel tap could be turned over to utilise a more economical paraffin mixture. Though bought ostensibly for bringing timber down from the hillside, the fitting of an attachment enabled the land to be levelled in the aftermath of the pigs, ready for rotovation.

Lots of stones had to be taken away from one particular patch, for this was the site on which the horses, in time gone by, had plodded round and round in a monotonous circle to rotate the millstones.

Now was the time of year to plant fruit trees so I dug out a trench along the southern facing walls of the barns, working whenever the weather was not too wet or windy, and I was not too miserably cold. Then, using many barrow loads of good well rotted muck that had been accumulated from the goat house and the rabbit pens, with a quantity of peat and a sprinkling of lime and bone meal, I was ready to see what the various nurseries had to offer.

The precise selection was carried out jointly for, just as I was looking forward to training my favourite dessert apples in espalier formations along the walls my wife was anticipating the plums and cooking apples she could collect from the small orchard I was creating nearby. We both agreed however, that no trees less than four years old be purchased, in order that we might sample our crop the following year and that pears be completely disregarded for they would probably take beyond our lifetime to reach fruition.

We knew that Christmas was not going to be quite the same that year but were certain that the two departed family members would have wished us to enjoy the festive season in their absence.

Happily we worked together with drawing pins and sticky tape until colourful paper decorations and balloons were festooned around the home. Then Fay hung a welcoming wreath of holly leaves with bright red berries on the outside of the front door, but at that point something went wrong . . .

"I just had a sudden pain across my chest" she said as she stumbled backwards against the wall. We spoke of indigestion, or the possible effect of the gusts of cold night air, little thinking that there could be any more serious involvement, but the next day while she sat in the surgery, her doctor picked up his telephone and arranged for an immediate electrocardiograph examination to be carried out. Subsequently a heart complication was diagnosed, and the lady who had so very much enjoyed the active country life and was so fastidious within her home had received one of nature's grimmest warnings, from now on there would have to be a great reduction in all her activities.

On New Year's Eve we retired quietly to bed long before the strains of "Auld Lang Syne" drifted across the Island and folks began dashing in and out of houses with the traditional pieces of lucky coal.

The Year we'd looked forward to was now over, for us the twelve months had not gone well, thank goodness there wouldn't be another Millennium for a thousand years.

CHAPTER 40

THE ONLY SOLUTION

THE New year was only a few days old when Tony was sent up to the attic to bring down a small suitcase, into which we quickly threw mummy's slippers, dressing gown, toothbrush, comb, hair-brush and so on, for a few minutes earlier our doctor had phoned to the sister on night duty at the hospital saying "I've got a lady way out in the country here, whom I want bringing in immediately".

Fay rested calmly on the settee, obeying instructions not to move. Since receiving an injection the acute pain across her chest had eased and she was already expressing concern for the welfare of Tony and I without her.

"Make sure he gets washed properly, and that he wears clean clothes for school", she was softy saying, as headlights at the top of the lane shone small square patterns of the window panes upon the curtains.

The ambulance driver swung clockwise round the winter bareness of the rose bed and reversed towards the house as his colleague jumped out and swung open the large rear doors.

Tony watched his mother carefully carried out of her home, placed gently inside the vehicle and covered with blankets. The doors were firmly closed, the engine re-started and when they drove her away the little fellow stood on the doorstep, he'd seen it all before, but his Grandad never came back to Ballaneddin.

Already long beyond his bedtime but obviously he couldn't just be left alone in the house so, in pyjamas and dressing gown he sat beside me as I drove behind the ambulance, there were no tears and any attempt to make light conversation with him seemed pathetic. So we travelled along in silence, following the rear lights ahead, each of us deeply troubled. Certainly no time was lost as we sped along that stretch of the T.T. course, but every mile towards the hospital seemed so much longer that evening.

In the reception area the pair of us sat quietly alone, each vacantly holding magazines in the reading position, until a young nurse requested me to follow her towards the womens' wards where, positioned at my wife's bedside were two types of electrical apparatus, each with a T.V. screen monitoring the most minute fluctuations in her condition and a couple of sinister looking black welding bottles stood ominously alongside with white collars clearly painted round their necks to indicate that the oxygen they contained was suitable for medical use, not unlike a pair of vicars I thought, but the situation was by no means funny.

After standing there for a few moments I was asked to withdraw but before I left the building the staff nurse wrote down my home telephone number and my wife's religion. The battle was now on, the situation was far beyond the simple reliance upon wholesome country living, a few herbal remedies and a bit of good luck: the skilled mechanics of modern medicine were now in charge, using their up-to-date equipment on our behalf. When driving homewards once more I most earnestly hoped they would send no ominous phone message through that night.

A few days later the crisis was thankfully over, the *Jump Leads* removed and our patient was sitting up taking an active part in the

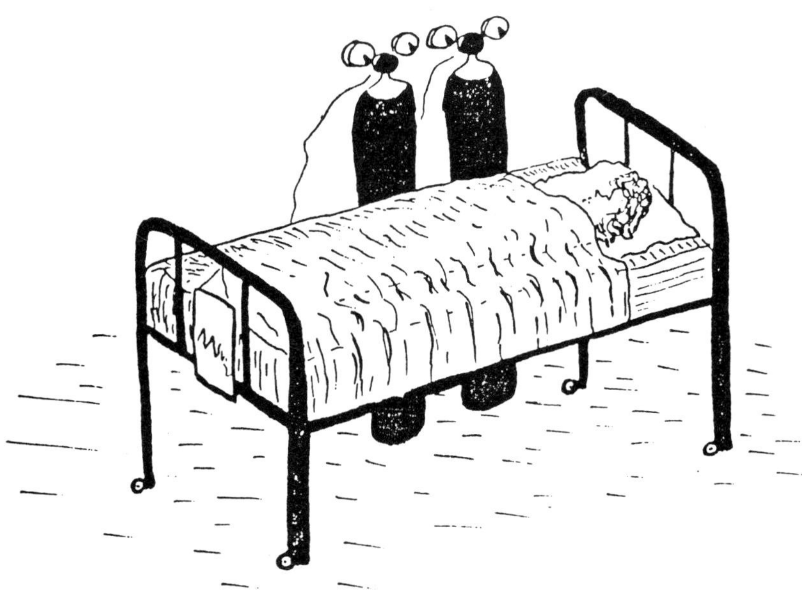

cheerful chatter of the Cottage Hospital ward, where, in spite of their misfortunes, the ladies each displayed their sense of humour.

During those anxious days I'd been inundated with messages of goodwill, offers of assistance and invitations for meals, so father and son had faired quite well during mother's enforced absence, but there were two particular household chores from which I had always disassociated myself, namely the baking of bread and the making of cheese. Consequently at the end of a fortnight we were not only missing that homely smell from an opened oven door, and longing to get our teeth into one of Mum's wholemeal crusts but were both almost awash with goats milk. Even those thieving half-wild pussy cats seemed to have become overfaced and were looking bloated. Whereas the poor dog was pining and quite bewildered, having hardly eaten anything during the course of this maternal absence, in spite of being privileged to sleep under the double bed that Tony and I now shared in consolation.

This was the time of year when people's thoughts were turned to holidays, their enthusiasm encouraged by the lavish publicity projects launched by an abundance of tour operators, all proclaiming the virtues of specific resorts and the facilities they had available.

Several thousand colourful holiday brochures had been despatched by the Isle of Man Tourist Board, each bearing a single line insertion indicating the details of our comfortably modernised farmhouse. Enquiries began arriving through the post and by telephone, calls being generally made either after six-o'clock (*cheaper rate*) or between one and two p.m. (*when the boss is out at lunch*). Unfortunately under the present circumstances, it was not possible to accept any bookings whatsoever, this was sad, for some of the people we'd been very happy to cater for the previous summer were wishing to stay with us again.

Caring for guests had been an interesting experience, particularly as the meals were so much appreciated, the farmstead admired, and our way of life so blatantly envied. One couple actually regarded the back-aching task of carrying sacks full of peat down the hillside as being a very pleasant vacational activity (why should I bother to discourage them) and two freshwater fishermen who came from London brought us gifts of most delicious rainbow trout each day, which made a much appreciated bonus.

The welcome news that Mummy was to come home shortly signalled the start of a major domestic operation. There were toys to be tidied away, dishes to wash, pans to scrub, sheets to change, clothing to be rammed into the washing machine and then pegged out to dry in the wind. Then a session of dusting and polishing that would have rendered the whole place ready for the most stringent of barrack room inspections.

Many thousands of people suffer the misfortune of having heart problems and have learnt to accept the situation and to adjust their lives accordingly. Fay was firstly to observe six weeks of careful convalescence within her own home, during which time she was under strictest instructions to "not even make herself a pot of tea", and, providing this necessity for complete rest was totally adhered to, there was no reason why she should not then begin to drive the car once more, carry out light housework and to enjoy many happy years in the future. Her rules for survival now were very simply, no physical exertion, no stress or anxiety, and to always carry her tablets close at hand.

Never again would we walk up the steep hillside together, to proudly look beyond our land and out across the sea. No more would we be able to carry out our combined operation of producing winter fuel with the chain saw across the cuddy. That wonderfully invigorating lifestyle she had so much enjoyed was now over for ever, replaced by the recognition that any deviation from the rules could bring about another seven mile journey of emergency.

Although I enjoyed my personal good fortune of having present fitness and ability, there came the nauseating doubt of just how many years could our self-sufficiency ideal be maintained more-or-less single-handedly?

There were disturbing thoughts that sooner or later we would become an old Derby and Joan couple shuffling slowly around in a house surrounded by nettles, thistles and bramble entanglements, with the nearby outbuildings in disuse and disrepair; for nature would very soon take back the paradise setting we had worked so hard for ten years to create.

There was only one solution and unfortunately the time had come . . .

We must relinquish our lovely Toy Town Kingdom for a tiny sack of gold, then attempt to live happily ever after in a smaller, more easily run, home . . . closer to the hospital!

CHAPTER 41

THE COUNT-DOWN

THE decision to sell Ballaneddin had been firmly agreed between us, but the parting would not be easy, it was not so much a question of buildings and land, it was an entire way of life, our life. We didn't want to sell, the situation had been forced upon us and when the first potential purchasers arrived I was aware of a slight resentment, these people were wandering around my home and intruding upon my privacy. It was to be hoped that eventually the transaction would be completed with some person who would appreciate all those minor refinements that had made the house a home, rather than some obnoxious personality who just happened to have the ability to write down the highest number on a piece of bank paper.

The old horse-drawn implements of earlier days were still lying around the premises and the Manx Museum officials were delighted to be given their free choice among the selection. When their lorry had been fully loaded with weighty items of outdated, hand-forged machinery, plus a quantity of rather dilapidated harness, I was pleased to think it was all to end in the Folk Museum, which surely was the rightful place, but the remainder were easily sold off to become gaily painted garden ornaments.

Endeavouring to support the wisdom of the decision that was to bring about such a great domestic upheaval we attempted to make a down-to-earth, non-sentimental appraisal of this back-to-nature living, based on ten years of practical experience.

The pleasure, the supreme personal satisfaction, was of course utterly beyond assessment but the basic pros and cons of home production needed deeper consideration. Tomatoes are so flavourful when picked straight off the plant, but by the time my unheated greenhouse produced its crop, shop prices had already reached rock-bottom. Cauliflowers all become ready around the same time, so half got thrown to the livestock. The first home-produced eggs had been such a novelty, collected warm and fresh, straight from the nest but latterly they had lost favour, to become just another incoming item that had to be dutifully incorporated within the weekly menu to avoid an accumulation.

A couple of friends, whose kitchen so often bore that appetizing aroma of family meals being prepared on a woodburning stove, once returned from holiday to speak in absolute delight of having done some baking in a straightforward electric oven, controlled heat at the turn of a switch, no sawing, chopping, fetching, carrying, lighting or cleaning out . . . What a luxury!

Goatsmilk, we had found to be very palatable, no, it isn't strongly flavoured (unless you happen to give the poor creature a diet of turnips and turnips) and has some definite nutritional advantages, but our dairy turnover fluctuated between feast and famine with goats being either heavily pregnant and dried up or producing a gallon a day. Why on earth we bothered to have three of them I just can't understand. Fay certainly made lots of delicious cheeses, in a variety of styles and herbal flavours but they had been so frequently beyond out household requirements and subsequently given away, or even recycled to the pigs. What gastronomic sacrilege!

Routine bread-baking sessions had certainly ensured that ample supplies were available for all-comers, but, so often loaves produced a couple of days previously were bypassed by the household and in due course became thrown into the farmyard for the hens, and there was always such an abundance of home produced meat on hand that this led to a rather excessive family consumption.

So, our initial theory that the ideal life should be of basic simplicity and domestic economy had become rather distort. Had we been working hard these years to live in extravagance, within the wasteful, modern, throw-away society we had so criticised?

The ideal purchasers for Ballaneddin would have been some younger couple wishing to carry out a similar way of living, though perhaps without the same indulgence, who would have taken over the entire established set-up with buildings, equipment and livestock. But nearly all the people who came to inspect were in the process of selling property, farms or even factories in England and wished to retire with a satisfactory income tax advantage, with no more commitment to livestock than maybe just a couple of riding horses.

The state of uncertainty, that every prospective house vendor understands, went on for weeks and was most detrimental to Fay's health till finally some apparently wealthy people came along who not only wished to make a purchase, they also arranged to acquire further acres nearby. We learnt that it was not their intention to carry out practical farming in the general manner but to bring over to the Island their own particular menagerie of rare species of sheep, together with two goats, two horses, a donkey and a cow, plus several cats and dogs. This would involve quite an expensive Noah's Ark transportation, but Mr. and Mrs. Noah seemed to have ample cash available and presumably they would employ local labour to look after their pets upon arrival.

A contract of sale was legally drawn up, our barn was filled with bales of hay at the Noahs' request and Fay was able to start choosing carpets and curtains for the house we hoped to move to near Ramsey.

Life would seem very empty without all my fur and feather farmyard friends to feed and care for and it was certainly with a most miserable reluctance that I entered the rabbit house carrying a short iron bar instead of the fresh greenery that the line of twenty little twitchy noses anticipated each time the door was opened. One by one they were gently lifted out, dispatched with instantaneous precision, skinned and cut into portions ready for freezing, until every cage was empty and I was alone in the strange stillness of the building where so often the breeding does had made cosy nests with hay and lined them with soft fur from their own bodies before giving birth to their litters.

Arrangements were made for the nanny goats to go to good homes, they had been our milk producing family pets for several years, each answering its name and jumping up onto the milking bench when requested, but their three young billy kids would

have to be disposed of. A baby male goat, at three months old is a little larger than a good sized hare and tastes like very tender lamb, but if left to mature would develop a definite goatee flavour.

I was glad to think that shortly this necessity for bloodshed would all be over, the killing of little animals that I'd bred and cared for and who'd shown me their affection in return, did not come easy. The usual procedure with the baby goats was to administer a very sharp hammer blow on the head. Followed by quick work with a good knife for bleeding and skinning. In the shortest space of time, that pretty little Bambi, whose playful antics, springing round the farmyard had been so amusing, was gone for ever.

Fay had once read an article that recommended the use of chloroform on little goats, so, when the next necessity arose I had visited the chemist and come away with a bottle of ether. The poor little victim bleated and struggled to get away from the unpleasant chemical fumes of the cotton wool pressed across its nostrils for several unpleasant moments before becoming limp.

The procedure had been less violent but much more prolonged and later we learnt that the poor animal had been uselessly sacrificed. The carcase it yielded was so impregnated with the pain killing vapour that, while cooking, the kitchen bore the smell of a dental clinic and each portion of meat tasted so strongly of cough mixture that even the dog and the cats declined to eat it.

The sentimental countdown towards the evacuation of Balla-neddin was well under way but still each appearance in the farm-yard brought a host of chickens and bantams fluttering across to greet me. As they gathered round my feet for a pocketful of corn it seemed so unfortunate that their friendly human was soon to become their executioner.

CHAPTER 42

PEE-CO

THE exchange of contracts and payment of deposit by Mr. and Mrs. Noah had now become long overdue and we began to lose confidence in their promised word. Then a further anxiety came upon us, this time from an entirely unexpected source.

One sunny afternoon Fay collected Tony out of school and drove into Ramsey, she left him to walk through the park with Pee-co our timid but well behaved young sheep dog on a lead; she was to meet me in town, then half an hour later the pair of us were to pick up Tony to go home.

This arrangement started a very unhappy series of events that were to upset the whole family, for inside the park, beside the boating lake, although several notices proclaimed that "DOGS MUST BE KEPT ON A LEAD", along bounded a large black labrador which promptly set about our poor Pee-co with a strong homosexual enthusiasm.

A short while later I found my ten-year-old Tony, pitifully holding the dog lead, on the other end of which was only an empty collar.

The young sheepdog had last been seen running at great speed out of the park entrance, quite understandable in the circumstances, *I would do the same myself*. We searched all round the town till darkness, but saw no sign of him whatsoever.

The next morning when I went downstairs and looked sadly at his empty basket my biggest worry was that he might get involved with bad company and become associated with mischief amongst the sheep. I have little sympathy myself for owners who allow their pets to roam loose at lambing time, apart from the obvious potential traffic hazard, and I appreciate that the use of a shot-gun has to be the final solution in extreme cases. The total injustice of the circumstances whereby my own innocent animal was now running loose without a collar or means of identification was very disturbing.

I went into Ramsey and drove round and round, asking about him time and time again. Fay telephoned Manx Radio and a request came over the air for any information but not until almost midnight, when we had gone to bed, did the phone ring. "My brother has just been walking his dog in the park and he's seen a black and white border collie there".

Quickly we dressed, woke Tony, wrapped a dressing gown around him, bundled him into the back of the car and set off to collect the family pet.

We drove slowly round the boating lake through the lines of palm trees and between the flower beds, stopping to whistle and call again and again. Fay whistles much more loudly than I do and we knew he would come if he was anywhere in earshot, but, having been in hospital only a few weeks previously suffering from a heart attack, it was so wrong for her to be getting upset like this and walking up and down the park in the cold air of one o'clock in the morning.

The next day Manx Radio very kindly again sent out their appeal for information and I toured round and round the Ramsey area, phoning home from time to time to see if Fay had any news. One of Tony's school friends did ring up, but by the time we reached the place he'd mentioned there was no dog in sight.

I made out notices, offering reward money and placed them in the windows of a couple of shops, it may seem silly to become emotionally involved over a mere dog, but this bright little fellow had become such a well loved member of our household.

Again, late at night, came word of a black and white border collie that had been seen hanging around the outside of the public houses in the north of the Island. A few phone calls later and we spoke to a lady who was now taking care of the stray. She gave a description, but said she would dearly like to keep the dog if this could possibly be arranged, but as the conversation continued we realised that this good lady had actually taken in this particular animal before our Pee-co's troubles had even begun.

For yet a third day we enjoyed the wonderful generosity of the local radio station and all their personnel were wondering where the dog could be. It was very frustrating. On one occasion we went along to a local glen and whistled, sure enough a black and white collie came through the trees but it belonged to someone else.

Phoning Manx Radio on the fourth day we told them how much their help had been appreciated, but surely their charity must have reached its limitation, so could we now have some spots over the air for which we were willing to pay. Prices were quoted and it was agreed that the following day there should be a fifteen second advert sent out six times. But of course our own resources had their limitations, already I'd driven over two hundred miles at a slow cruising speed round the Ramsey area, but all these activities would soon have to be called to a halt.

The cumulative effect of all this publicity began to bring results. A lady who had been meeting her husband off a fishing boat at one o'clock in the morning thought she'd seen our four legged friend by the Swing Bridge. Another fisherman had seen a "very spritely young collie" on the harbour wall. One group of workers said that if they caught him during the day they would leave him tied to the concrete mixer for me to collect. The gardeners in the park said they would phone as soon as they spotted him. Everyone was so very helpful but I think the border collie must be the most popular breed upon the Island, almost every farm seems to have one or quite often two.

Fay picked up the phone once and a man's voice came over, "I've caught your dog lady, I've got him tied here with a piece of string". Unfortunately, a detailed description just didn't tally with our missing friend.

We laughed together at the thought of all the loose black and white dogs in the Island being rounded up and tied with string, but we both really felt rather wretched, not knowing whether he was dead or alive as each day went by.

We decided that as so many calls were coming from the Ramsey area and, knowing his timid nature, he could perhaps be in hiding most of the day, coming out after dark to see what food could be found around the backs of the hotels and cafes.

On the seafront we spoke to one of the Coastguards who had been on duty overnight. "Very early this morning, before anyone was about, I saw a young sheepdog chasing seagulls along the north shore" he said, raising our hopes yet again. "Go up in the look-out tower and see if you can spot him now."

I climbed the steps and into what was then the nerve centre of all marine rescue operations in the Irish Sea. There were two uniformed officers, occupying themselves with various items of electronic apparatus when I walked in. Half the wall area was covered with charts and data while the rest was taken up by large windows looking out to sea and along the coastline in each direction.

"I'm looking for a dog", I said, immediately wondering to myself what was the significance of the term dog-watch.

They both spoke of the radio broadcasts they'd already heard (who hadn't by now) and promptly began to scour the coast with their powerful optical equipment, but without success.

The only way to catch sight of our elusive little animal would be to stay on the quayside all night and to keep a particularly sharp look-out in the early hours.

We drove a motor-caravan into town, searched around till dusk, bought some chips, brewed some tea, and settled down for an all-night vigil. We had enjoyed a long dry spell of weather but now the rain came, it absolutely poured all night. At about half-past-four however, it began to come daylight, so I sat in the driving seat peering steadfastly through the windscreen, switching the wipers on frequently and occasionally driving around just to warm the engine and gain that little extra comfort from it. I must have seen every stray dog and every pussy in that entire area.

Back home once more we had the cold awareness of failure, even now accepting the fact that our world would not stop going round just because we'd lost a dog. Then the phone rang, it was a call from the police. "A lady rang in earlier this morning to say she'd seen an animal of your description up at the Gooseneck, she'd tried to catch it but it was very frightened."

The "Gooseneck" is the name of one of the dangerous bends where the T.T. course makes its way over the mountain, it's about six hundred feet above sea level and derives its name from the actual shape of the roadway.

I set off once more, but this time with no confidence whatsoever, I'd followed up every clue so far and was getting tired and frustrated, but as the lady had bothered to make her phone call at least I should bother to go and look around for a couple of minutes. The rain had now reduced to drizzle and as I climbed I drove through patches of mist and switched my lights on, how could I possibly find a dog on a mountain in weather like this? I had the feeling I was wasting my time, a couple of hours in bed would have done me more good.

I couldn't safely stop on the actual twisting Gooseneck, so I carried on further where the roadway straightened out, then pulled in close to the dry-stone wall. I came to a complete stop directly opposite a tumbled down gap in the stonework, that had been crossed with wire to retain the sheep. I switched off the engine and pulled on the handbrake, automatically looking through the opening on my left. Just a few feet away, there was a black and white dog lying flat upon the wet grass, not just anybody's black and white dog, this really was PEE-CO! Yes, it was our PEE-CO!

I think the first feeling that registered was absolute surprise, the joy came fractionally later. I'd spent five days searching, sighted dozens of dogs, become resigned to failure, then suddenly here was the absolutely unexpected.

I jumped out and ran round the car, but Pee-co had already got up and was limping away into the mist.

"PEE-CO! PEE-CO!" I shouted, not particularly in joy, more in urgency, lest he should disappear from view. He stopped, he was definitely my dog, the black and white markings were exactly as I had been describing over and over again, but his bedraggled coat was completely soaked and his wet tail, with its white tip, dragged onto the ground.

"Come on my boy, come on then" I said, as calmly as I could while climbing the wall. Even while doing this I felt a wave of thankfulness to see that only a short distance away the sheep were peacefully grazing with their lambs afoot, he had caused them no concern.

Never before have I seen any animal in such an utter state of exhaustion, he was surely on the very verge of collapse. He smelled my hands, looked up to my face and gave very faint whimpers.

I got him into the car but he was completely bewildered. Normally so bright-eyed and responsive but now just vacant and confused — I wondered if he'd been run over.

Continuing over the mountain road then down the valley towards home, passing through the village I stopped at the phone box, pressed my coin in the slot and Fay burst into tears when she heard me say "I've got him!"

Then I warned her that he seemed to be in a state of shock and that she and Tony should restrain themselves lest they overwhelmed him with their welcome.

I spoke very calmly to him as we drove along, but it was not until we turned off the road, between those two stone pillars at Ballaneddin that he showed any interest and it was only then when he saw mother and son standing in the doorway did a slight movement at the tip of his tail show that he knew he was at home at last

We dried him in the kitchen and made a careful examination for any injury and came to the conclusion that for the last five days the poor creature had been trying to find his way home. The tough layers of skin on the pads of his feet were worn right through, he was almost walking on raw flesh. While we were wondering if he could possibly be making himself at home on someone else's hearth rug he had actually been running around for mile after mile desperately searching for the only home he knew.

Fay phoned through to Manx Radio with our wonderful news, and within minutes there was an announcement that the saga of the missing sheepdog had reached a happy ending.

We were certainly very grateful to the Broadcasting staff, to the Police, the Coastguards, the M.S.P.C.A. and to all those wonderfully considerate people who rang up with information about almost every black and white dog that was loose for many miles around, but not one solitary person had even mentioned the reward and the lady who sighted him at the Gooseneck had not even given her name.

CHAPTER 43

BREAKING POINT

SIX months had now gone by since Fay came back to us from hospital and we had reached our decision and resigned ourselves to the fact that the most sensible, though heart breaking thing to do, under the drastically changed circumstances, was to put Balla-neddin up for sale.

During that length of time the Island's half dozen or so Estate Agents had each been along, taking photos and then giving us the satisfaction of reading the glowing reports they produced of the extremely desirable country residence, as they announced to all and sundry through the local papers that the property was "on the market".

"Should sell well" they had said, each one hoping to grab his one-and-a-half per cent commission, permissible under Manx ruling, before any of his contempories.

Nobody had been given the authority to plant one of those "FOR SALE" boards at the bottom of the lane, for we wished the agents to establish first of all that any persons they sent along could at least be regarded as genuine potential buyers.

The Island is a wonderfully law-abiding little territory but an Estate Agents notice is more or less an invitation, or at least an excuse, for all and sundry to wander around.

Time and time again, we'd picked up the telephone "Will it be convenient for a certain Mr. and Mrs. Moneybags to view your property, in an hours time?"

This would trigger off the household cry of "Action Stations" and a hectic sixty minutes of dusting, tidying, polishing, ramming Tony's toys under his bed, hurling the cats out of the door and banishing the bewildered dog to the end of a chain in the yard.

Then answering the front door chimes with all the calm and relaxed charm as occupants of a peaceful, easily-run country residence, where dirty pots and pans never pile up in the kitchen sink, and no-one could possibly throw filthy, muddy wellies into the porchway.

In the earlier months we carried out quite regular conducted tours, up and down the stairs, explaining with pride our complete restoration of ten years ago, supported with the "before and after" photos, pointing out all the electrical sockets and praising the efficiency of a brand new solid fuel continental cooking stove that we'd just installed to replace our original old Solid Sally. The party would then be led outside, where we wandered in and out of the buildings, till all eyes were directed towards the hillside, where ten acres of woodland could be casually hinted as being, "Possibly enough fuel for a lifetime". This remark was most enthusiastically received by folks who had probably never even picked up a chain saw, or handled a felling axe in their lives. To me, the production of a hundredweight of logs every day now meant quite a lot of backache.

Returning to the house for further discussion I would produce the tenancy agreement whereby the young farmer living nearby had the use of the reclaimed land on top of the hill, in return for four fat lambs per annum, which we put into our deep-freeze. This invariably brought enthusiasm from the lady viewers, who straightaway visualised a splendid selection of lamb chops etc. all pre-packed and ready to serve their requirements. What astonishment there would have been if each lady had been expected to help her husband lift the animals into the back of a van, alive and kicking, wet and smelly, then to drive the sixteen miles to the

abattoir, while they peed all over the van floor and steamed up the windscreen.

Each visit would take up at least an hour, during which time Fay would invariably serve coffee and biscuits for which there was usually a genteel expression of thanks followed by an assurance that the property had been found very interesting indeed and that the agent would be contacted.

One such interested party spoke of housing his collection of vintage cars inside the farm buildings but a Harley Street specialist thought them ideal for conversion into a private clinic. A solicitor from London would make his servants quarters inside the barn and another solicitor wished to commute between the Island and his Cheshire practice by private aircraft. One lady expressed her absolute adoration of the huge chestnut trees growing round the homestead, another asked if it were possible to have them all cut down. There was one couple over from America and another came from Norway who asked permission to take photographs and left us wondering if they'd simply come over to compile an illustrated survey of life on the Isle of Man (which has of course so many historical associations with the Scandinavian nations).

We treated everyone with courtesy and patience even the gentleman sporting a public school tie who talked such a lot and seemed more interested in the contents of my whisky decanter than my property. This was all very frustrating.

We only needed one customer to buy Ballaneddin in order to change to that entirely different way of life that was now so necessary for Fay's future. Each visit brought tension, so much uncertainty, will they, won't they? Are they genuine or are they just passing the time at our expense? How can one tell?

Mr. and Mrs. Noah were the only people who had actually got down to the harsh reality of the amount of cash involved, we'd agreed a figure, they'd arranged to purchase further acres nearby, four hundred bales of hay were already stored in our barn at their request and yet, nothing whatsoever had been signed to ensure that they would carry our their side of the bargain. This was very worrying, week after week went by, the contracts had been drawn up but their own vital signatures had not been added.

We knew that property sales in the Isle of Man and in England too had been brought almost to a standstill by virtue of the very high interest rates but this gave us no consolation, particularly as we were aware that no less than twenty-eight farms were now for sale on the Island.

Every night before falling asleep our conversation was like a housing committee meeting. The continuous question mark hung over the signing of the contract, will they? won't they? So much so that by now, when I awoke at about five o'clock I felt delighted to find that I'd slept so long, but then Fay would move, whisper "Are you awake Denys?" and the meeting was again in progress.

One morning in July we lay in bed speculating on what phone calls the day would bring. What would the postman push through? Then I got dressed, pottered about downstairs till seven, when I took Fay a cup of tea.

"I've got a pain in my chest", she said, very quietly. She'd already put one of the special little tablets under her tongue, so I just held her hand and sat by the bed for a few minutes.

"The pain's a bad one, and it's just not going, I think I need the Doctor."

Our family Doctor was away on holiday, but I was straightaway through to one of his colleagues.

"Give her another tablet, if the pain hasn't gone in ten minutes ring again and I'll come out to you right away", was the instruction.

When the finger of my wrist watch reached the tenth minute I quietly asked if she still had pain. Her head nodded slightly and I ran downstairs to the telephone again.

The Doctor lost no time travelling those seven miles from Ramsey speeding along the deserted road where the countryside had not long come to life. The sun was shining, "Good morning", I said, as he stepped inside, but immediately realised the stupidity of my automatic salutation, for our little family there was nothing good whatsoever about that particular summer morning.

He checked his patient's pulse and blood pressure, then gave an injection that was so effective that within a minute a great expression of relief came over her face.

"Thank goodness that's gone", she said, but we both knew full well that her troubles were by no means over.

"We must treat this as a coronary, until such time as tests prove otherwise", the Doctor told me, then, putting down the telephone he added, "the ambulance will get here in fifteen minutes . . ."

Tony was awake and out of bed by now so I told him to bring the small suitcase from the attic and his mother softly told us exactly where to find each nightie she wanted packing, also her dressing gown, bedjacket, soap, flannel, toothbrush, toothpaste, talcum powder, etc., and as before she was so wonderfully calm and sensible about the situation. Then I saw the ambulance come down the lane to Ballaneddin for the third time within the last few months, round the rose bed it drove, then backed towards the front of the house and the rear doors were opened, then up the stairs went the two attendants carrying a folding chair and blanket.

With gentle efficiency their early patient was soon in the chair, wrapped securely in the blanket and being carried down the stairway.

"Soon have you there Love", said the driver, with the tender cheerfulness of an experienced hospital worker, with her welfare very much at heart.

Tony and I were going to follow immediately behind in the car but it was suggested I wait for half an hour or so to let the hospital staff get her comfortably bedded down.

From the door step we watched the ambulance drive away down the lane, then through the old stone gate posts, turning to the right onto the roadway, and go speeding towards Ramsey. The driver would waste no time travelling along that T.T. course he knew so well.

We closed the door and both sat side by side at the bottom of the stairs, with arms around each other. Not a word was said, but both our cheeks were moist.

We knew she was such a good Mummy and such a good wife, it just didn't seem fair that she should be so poorly.

CHAPTER 44

A DECADE IS OVER

YET another crisis had fallen heavily across our household. News of the misfortune quickly spread further afield and sympathetic calls were soon coming in even from well-wishers to whom normal communications had gradually been reduced to symbolic Christmas greetings. The grim significance of that ominous word "Coronary" had been passed around, producing the rather exasperating enquiry, "Is it a bad one?" Personally, I'd never heard of a good one and felt very inclined to say so.

In a hospital room bedecked with flowers and get well cards Fay once more thankfully weathered the storm and then began the gradual day by day progression from a privileged half hour sitting-up-in-bed position to a similar duration of occupying a chair alongside.

The visiting times and procedure were already familiar, paper handkerchiefs to be purchased, messages to be conveyed and fruit to be replenished. The faces of nearest and dearest, visiting other patients became recognisable by their frequency, the majority of whom would take up positions in the waiting room, quietly thumbing through the magazines, continually glancing up towards the wall clock ready to surge forward down the passageway to the respective wards the instant the staff nurse gave her authorisation. The remainder would stand outside in the open air until they saw the waiting room being vacated, then hastily stamp out the forbidden cigarettes and scurry along in pursuit of the main party.

We were very thankful when Mummy was home with us once more but this time all doubts and each reluctant thought about selling our home were completely discarded, the need to move nearer to town, in smaller and more easily run accommodation had become an urgent necessity.

Unfortunately we were soon to learn that after five months of promises, Mr. and Mrs. Noah had changed their minds about coming over to the Island (maybe they thought that the rainfall in England was not going to be all that bad after all). The barn-full of hay they'd had delivered for their boatload of livestock, but not paid for, had to be carted away again, with the exception that is of one bale, into which a frightened hare had committed suicide, to become a putrid mass of decaying flesh and seething maggots. Dragging it aside for burning I felt that somehow the less savoury aspects of rural activity were becoming more noticeable. Was the "good life" beginning to lose its bloom?

Certainly, many of the routine duties that had previously been carried out between us with absolute vigour and enjoyment, had now become unavoidable chores. A frustrating autumn turned to winter, which involved sloshing round in muddy wellingtons putting down portions of poison bait for the wretched long tailed vermin as the weather became colder and they took refuge in the outbuildings.

Each morning the kitchen stove had to be cleaned out and the tray of ashes removed. Now however, there was the awareness of how frequently it was either raining or gusts of wind blew the stuff into my face as it was emptied.

Worries about slates that might have slid off the barn roof during an overnight storm and thoughts of how many woodworms might be silently chomping their destructive tunnels though the timbers beneath, added to the overall unrest. At one stage of their life cycle these insects fly around in quest of new territory. Within the house itself, most of the timbers had been rendered very unappetising, but nevertheless it was prudent to maintain a vigil and periodically search every inch of the attic area with a flashlight.

The outbuildings were festooned with cobwebs and at one time I had optimistically hoped that all '*flying woodworms*' would become trapped and devoured by the spiders. Unfortunately, this just did not happen. On the contrary, the first indication of the larvae's presence was often when sighting the tell-tale deposits of fine, light coloured powder actually suspended in the cobwebs that hung below the boreholes.

The property market both in England and in the Isle of Man was said to be almost at a standstill. Our frustration and total uncertainty about the future was turning to depression with the knowledge that without continual maintenance so much of the old world charm we'd developed around our farm house setting would easily slip away. Without goats the paddock could become a jungle; without pigs the styes would fill up again with nettles and without attention given to the fine holly trees that lined the driveway they could become strangled by the ivy and the brambles.

"FOR SALE" notices were conspicuous all over the Island and property advertisements occupied several pages of the local papers. Christmas passed in quiet anxiety, with the remote consolation that lots of other people were suffering the complications of recession in various forms, through not necessarily with our particular medical involvement.

With the coming of Spring and at the first suitably dry spell, I busied myself with brushing down and re-whitewashing walls and outbuildings, then clearing our greenhouse in readiness for the tomato plants.

A few people were now on the Island looking round properties for sale but it was difficult to take their enquiries very seriously, until one day a couple announced that they'd received bundles of literature from the various estate agents and had deposited the whole lot in the dustbin with the exception of a short-list of four possibilities.

Unlike the dozens who had tramped in and out of every room inside our home during the previous twelve months, these people were, in due course, to become the new occupants of Balla-neddin.

The realisation dawned rather slowly and sadly that we were actually going to vacate the home we so cherished. Not until the furniture van was loaded, could I really believe that the lovely home, the stone outbuildings and all that territory forming our little kingdom was passing into strangers hands.

The following day, we returned to Ballaneddin, no longer our home, just an empty house. Wandering from room to room we saw the impressions of our heavier possessions outlined on the carpets and the shadowy shapes of removed pictures faintly picked out on the walls.

With some kind neighbourly assistance Fay spent the entire day vacuuming and polishing from top to bottom, "Always leave a place just as you would like to find it", she had said, but unfortunately showed complete disregard for her doctor's orders in the process.

Out in the farmyard, for the last time, I collected the eggs from a surviving handful of hens, which were scheduled to come under new ownership, filled their nest boxes with clean hay and topped their food hopper to capacity. In the greenhouse I had planted tomatoes, then carefully watered and manured them over recent weeks though knowing I would perhaps not be there to enjoy the fruit. The crop was quite heavy and just beginning to ripen, I gave them water, then went to the wood store and chopped a quantity of dry kindling sticks.

The incoming residents would, at that time, be motoring up to the north of England to board the midnight boat that would get them to the Island in the early hours of the morning. They would be tired when they eventually reached their new home but they would find not only coal and logs in the bunker, sticks in readiness by the stove but also a greetings card, a colourful flower arrangement and the traditional packet of table salt to wish them both good fortune and happiness for the future.

We closed the front door, turned our backs on Ballaneddin and did not look behind. Ironically, it was Fay who was obliged to drive through the line of holly trees for the final time. I'd had a slight mishap and had been limping around on crutches for the previous couple of weeks.

Although, through unfortunate circumstances the ultimate decision had been virtually forced upon us, we were fully aware that sooner or later we would both have got beyond the ability to fulfill the physical requirements of an active semi-self-supporting existence.

The time had come to make a move into a less demanding life-style. We'd enjoyed a wonderful decade, learning to appreciate all aspects of a rural environment and gained the satisfying knowledge that within our period of ownership several acres of desolate Manx shrubland had been transformed into good productive pasture.

We were taking with us a wealth of experience and a host of memories.

IT HAD BEEN A GOOD LIFE, A VERY GOOD LIFE!

ALPHABETICAL AFTER-THOUGHTS

from the many hours spent in the kitchen

BUTTERMILK. Is the liquid remaining after the butterfat has been removed from milk by churning. Take your own bottle to the dairy and have it filled for a few coppers. A refreshing cheese flavoured drink when taken cold from the fridge. Goes well into coleslaw, makes good cottage cheese and is excellent to use when baking scones and sponge cakes.

CHĖVALINE. Not a Frenchman, who apparently has his name over a chain of butcher's shops, from where, many a self-catering holiday maker has no doubt purchased prime steaks and thoroughly enjoyed a subsequent meal back at the apartment or camping site. Blissfully unaware that, between sips of reasonably priced red wine, the family have been enthusiastically devouring succulent mouthfuls of man's-best-friend.

Anyhow, those choice horse-meat steaks are not the heartbreaking remains of some sad person's old faithful companion, which has clip, clopped, slowly into a knacker's yard and flicked its ears, pathetically trying to catch and obey a final word of command. On the contrary, large quantities of young tender, purposebred stock are imported from South America and Poland, similar to the international shipments comprising carcasses of beef and lamb.

CHICKWEED. Spreads about the garden and gets into the greenhouse. A small amount is said to be beneficial in salad, full of iron – tried it, not impressed, more acceptable to the livestock.

COD'S HEAD. Norwegian fisherman's way. The cheeks and top of the head are carefully filleted away from the skull in one piece, popped into the frying pan, sizzled on one side and then the other. Delightful, sweetest piece of the fish.

COMFREY. Herbal tradition for healing wounds has been established over many centuries. Grows easily in the garden. Phenomenal claims are made of its agricultural use in Soviet countries. Leaves lining a potato trench give good results. Stand a bucket of leaves covered with water in the greenhouse for a couple of weeks and it will smell like vintage urine, but when decanted alongside tomato plants it certainly does them a power of good.

DANDELION. Drop a slate over a growing plant and in a short while tender young blanched shoots can be added to salad. Dandelion flowers, with boiling water, sugar, a little orange rind and yeast can make an interesting country wine. Pick the flowers away from the contaminated roadside, on a sunny day, when they are fully opened, for it is only the bright yellow petals that are used, not the supporting greenery.

DOG FISH. Look like small sharks and are plentiful in the Irish Sea. They are known as Huss, Flake and even Rock Salmon elsewhere. Removing the very tough dark grey skin looks easy only when it is being done by an expert. The large white sections of boneless flesh can be used in fish pies and many other dishes.

ECONOMY MEAL for next to nothing. Boil a big cod's head in pan 'til all the skin and flesh falls away, lift out the bone and add your own selection of herbs and vegetables. Cheap and satisfying, but don't serve the eyeballs.

EGGS are incorporated in a countless number of good food recipes. If you're not too successful at separating the yolk use a tea-strainer, only the white will run through and if in the course of preparation your hard boiled eggs have become confused amongst some that are uncooked, just give each a quick spin on a flat surface and stop it abruptly, then release. Any liquid content will endeavour to slosh it's way around and the egg will move.

FRESH FISH. A good housekeeping approach for those privileged to live in a coastal region, is to seek and buy as a spontaneous purchase that which has been freshly landed and at its tasteful best, rather than have a pre-determined species in mind for the family menu.

The flesh must be firm, slimy, slippery but not floppy. Scales must be close-fitting, not falling loose and eyes still bright and clear rather than with a dead-pan, morning-after expression. However, even if the smaller fishing boats have been storm-bound for a couple of days, one can still select something appropriate that has been caught in deeper waters and brought back by the large refrigerated, ocean going, factory vessels.

FUEL. Unless timber and peat is freely available, and the procuration time of little consequence, the economic advantages of homemade bread, slow casseroles and such like are considerably reduced.

Re-cycling newspapers in the form of papier-maché logs is carried out in some homes on a tiny scale. If however, a newspaper delivery service was incorporated, whereby papers were to be planted through letter boxes daily, for a fee, but subsequently harvested in bundles, say once a week, without charge, a cost-free stock-pile could soon be established. Furthermore, if mechanical assistance could carry out the shredding and pulping operation, and if access could be gained to give-away supplies of such combustibles as coal-dust, saw-dust and wood shavings for adding to the slushy mass, together with chopped straw, then suddenly, the entire log-making project would become an exciting, profit making venture. (Wait a minute, how are you going to dry the sodden things?)

GARLIC is easy to grow, just push a few cloves in the ground in the spring and they will multiply. Its beneficial qualities are indisputable, having been in use medicinally for about five thousand years. It's known to prevent blood clotting in race horses and to have counteracted diabetes in rabbits but it is only over comparatively recent years that medical research has begun to bear out old wives' tales that it was good for the heart, apparently lowering the level of fat in the system and keeping blood pressure down.

HAGGIS. That supreme national dish, the Scotish Super Sausage. An indisputable credit to a nation with that canny gift of making the best out of so very little. In its simplest form is a sheep's belly, rammed full of minced-up heart, lungs, liver, black pepper, oatmeal and onions. Very savoury and very satisfying.

HANDS. Always wash thoroughly before preparing food. Never joke with guests that you enjoy kneading the homemade bread because it gets your fingernails so clean.

ICE CUBES. Can make a jelly cool down quickly if you're running short of time and are certainly most convenient for watering plants that hang from baskets about your head.

INK FISH. Calamari, Squid, look very much like baby octopus but have ten tenticles instead of only eight. Wash clean, extract the one flat flexible bone, tenderize with a mallet or simply achieve the same breakdown in structure by boiling inside a pressure cooker, cut into strips and use in either hot or cold dishes.

INSIDE-OUTWARD COOKING by micro-wave is like rubbing your cold hands together to make them warm and has brought in a new exciting era of food preparation.

JELLY. When a jar of pickled beetroot is mixed into a raspberry jelly and allowed to set, the result is a surprisingly pleasant sweet and sour creation.

JOGGING. Varying amounts of exercise undertaken by family members seem a common sense requirement of any health preserving routine. Yet, whenever one sees a docile household pussycat, lazily sleeping its way through a lifetime of domesticated comfort, one is aware that the very same creature still has the ability, with split-second timing, to streak across the garden and with savage instinct snatch some inoffensive sparrow, or to make a standing jump several times its body height, and to run vertically up trees and fences. This supreme feline agility seems to be based on complete relaxation, plus an occasional full length stretch when awakening. The pussy cat doesn't go jogging to keep fit, but of course, she doesn't smoke, over eat, ever get intoxicated or even worry about the future either.

KIPPERS. These are herrings which have been slit down the middle and hung upon tenterhooks in a smoke filled area. Their unmistakable aroma, detected when returning from the farmyard and kicking off muddy boots outide the kitchen door early on a cold winter morning, certainly sets one's flavour buds awash. They may even be blended with a quantity of cod to produce a paté closely resembling smoked salmon.

LEEKS. Boil double the quantity for immediate requirements, then you can serve half with todays' hot meal and the remainder tomorrow, straight from the fridge, with a vinaigrette dressing as a very refreshing and palatable starter course.

LEMON. If only a few drops of juice are needed, why not squeeze the remainder into plastic ice-cube containers and freeze for another time?

LIVER. Sometimes a litle tough and slightly bitter when served. My own preference is to slice, sizzle very briefly on both sides in butter, then to eat immediately, very rare, tender as marshmallow, gory but delectable.

MARINATING. Meat and fish can be preserved, tenderised and greatly improved in flavour by the simple principle of soaking in a specific liquid e.g. brine, soya sauce, yoghurt, wine and so on. Thus presenting a vast range of extremely savoury, exotic but inexpensive dishes with countries of origin very far beyond the British Isles.

NEW POTATOES. Straight from the soil, with a sprig of mint, a pinch of salt and a blob of butter are hard to beat. Probably the most economical way to cultivate this eagerly anticipated vegetable delicacy is beneath a black polythene sheet. Utilizing a peep and take technique, but leaving the remainder to fully mature.

ONIONS. Absolutely essential in a multitude of gastronomic preparations and are said to have been the staple diet of those folk who built the Pyramids. Sliced apple and onion sandwiches make an interesting variation in the picnic basket.

OXTAIL SOUP. Surely one of the tastiest of soups but unfortunately, when the tail is purchased, the meat to bone ratio is such that it seems to render this "end" product comparatively expensive.

POTATO. The wholesome, fortifying tubers of the potato plant play such an important part, throughout Europe today, as an item of food, that it is difficult to realize that this vegetable has only been under widespread cultivation for a couple of centuries or so, having originally been brought over from South America earlier on, as an ornamental plant. It is never eaten raw by mankind, but at least a slice can be used to take the marks off window panes and mirrors.

There are very many different methods whereby the humble

potato may be prepared and presented, but have you ever thought of making a hole right through the centre, inserting a sausage, then baking in the microwave?

QUEENIES. This is the name given to the smaller variety of scallop shell fish that are dredged in vast numbers from the seabed off the Manx coastline and destined for the gourmet tables of London, Paris and even further afield.

SEAGULLS generally lay a clutch of three eggs and each Spring these were a much sort-after delicacy up to quite recent years. The rural logic applied when collecting was that when you see one egg only, don't touch it and the bird will come back. If you find two eggs just take one, it will be fresh and she'll still come back. Should you come across a completed set of three eggs don't disturb them for they can be up to three weeks old and very nearly due to hatch out.

SPAGHETTI. Basically flour and eggs and can be made by hand. Quite fascinating to watch an expert take hold of a hefty dollop of dough and bang it down upon the table a few times to elongate its form. Then to bend it double and holding each end go bang, bang, bang, stretching all the time. Double again so now four sagging portions are going up in the air and whack! down onto the surface. Stretching, stretching all the time, double again so that eight thick sausages, two foot long are now being whammed up and down. Another multiplication makes into sixteen thin sausages and the gymnastics are beginning to make sense. Double and bang, double and bang making more and more lengths, that are getting thinner and thinner until the traditionally accepted dimension is reached and over a hundred greyish looking boot-laces lie across the table.

The dough has to be of a precise consistency and the table dusted with flour at all times. Not an easy technique to master, try it yourself and probably end up with eight clumsy looking lengths of irregular shaped rope, or, at best, a kitchen that resembles a vandalised telephone exchange.

TARTAR SAUCE. An emulsion of egg yolks and oil is known as MAYONNAISE and can greatly enhance an immense range of cold refreshments. If however, a small quantity of finely chopped cocktail gherkins, capers and chives are added, the name TARTAR SAUCE is then given and its utilization is extended much further afield.

In Holland I have even bought a take-away bag of chips which, instead of having been splattered with the customary salt and vinegar, the vendor has politely offered "help yourself" tartar sauce.

UNPLEASANT BREATH after eating garlic or raw onions can be counteracted a little by the chlorophyl obtained from slowly chewing a sprig of parsley.

UNUSUAL PREPARATIONS of food have always aroused my interest, whether it has been watching a New Zealander calmly dip a piece of bread into a saucer of milk before frying it with bacon, eggs and slices of green unripe tomatoes, or seeing a Turkish fellow chop raw onions then pour over such a great quantity of salt that the pieces were completely buried. The latter process turned out to be an excellent procedure, for the dry mineral extracted the onion juice, taking away the raw sting to such an extent that when the procedure has been carried out a couple of times, with warm water rinses and draining in between, the finished product could be pleasantly incorporated into various yoghurt based Asian delicacies.

VINEGAR. It is so easy to make pickled onions, pickled cabbage and suchlike at home, but never have any exposed vinegar about when you are making your homemade wines, the lot can be easily ruined.

WATER. People can exist without food for many days, but survival totally without liquid is reduced to a limited number of hours. As abundant supplies of clean water are normally available nowadays it must be a good routine to ensure that the human plumbing system is well and truly flushed clear of impurities as regularly as possible, even with the flavour of a few hops now and again.

WEEDS. Innocent little plants growing in the wrong place at the wrong time.

WELSH RAREBIT? Seems a rare name to give a piece of toast with cheese and mustard smeared over it.

WINDFALL APPLES. Pick them up off the ground, wash, and chop into small pieces, or, better still pop them into an emulsifier, complete with skin, core, pips and stalks to reduce into a sloppy mush. Cover with water and stir every day to produce an insipid drink. Add sugar and raisins, leave to ferment in a warm place. Bottle as a moorish apple wine after about three months.

XMAS PUDDING. This is a deeply traditional once-a-year dish steeped in cherished memories of childhood and not to be trifled with. Don't risk a festive failure on the Great Day of Goodwill . . . use the recipe from a good cookery book.

YEAST. At the stage of breadmaking when the ingredients have been thoroughly mixed by energetic kneading, there comes a necessary time-lapse, when the dough must stand in a slightly warm, draughtproof and dustproof position, during which the yeast content causes the mixture to "rise", to double its volume. There is no better place for this to happen than inside an amply large plastic bag. (You could even stand it on top of the television and then watch two programmes at the same time.)

YORKSHIRE PUDDING. Surely the only culinary masterpiece that can have a gravy poured over in the main savoury course and be followed by a covering of syrup as a sweet.

ZEALOT. An individual who zealously produces food the hard way, gaining immense satisfaction, even when it's much cheaper at the supermarket.